Mindfulness and the Art *of* Managing Anger

OTHER TITLES IN THIS SERIES:-

The Art of Mindful Baking

The Art of Mindful Birdwatching

The Art of Mindful Gardening

The Art of Mindful Silence

The Art of Mindful Singing

The Art of Mindful Walking

Einstein and the Art of Mindful Cycling

Galileo and the Art of Ageing Mindfully

Happiness and How it Happens

The Heart of Mindful Relationships

The Joy of Mindful Writing

The Mindful Art of Wild Swimming

The Mindful Man

Mindful Pregnancy and Birth

Mindfulness and Compassion

Mindfulness and Music

Mindfulness and Surfing

Mindfulness and the Art of Drawing

Mindfulness and the Art of Urban Living

Mindfulness and the Journey of Bereavement

Mindfulness and the Natural World

Mindfulness at Work

Mindfulness for Black Dogs and Blue Days

Mindfulness for Unravelling Anxiety

The Mindfulness in Knitting

Zen and the Path of Mindful Parenting

Mindfulness and the Art *of* Managing Anger
Meditations on Clearing the Red Mist

Mike Fisher

Leaping Hare Press

This paperback edition published in the UK in 2018 by
Leaping Hare Press
An imprint of The Quarto Group
The Old Brewery, 6 Blundell Street
London N7 9BH, United Kingdom
T (0)20 7700 6700 F (0)20 7700 8066
www.QuartoKnows.com

First published in hardback in 2012

Text copyright © 2012 Mike Fisher
Design and layout copyright © 2017 Quarto Publishing plc

All rights reserved. No part of this book may be reproduced or transmitted in any form or by any means, electronic or mechanical, including photocopying, recording, or by any information storage and retrieval system, without written permission from the copyright holder.

British Library Cataloguing-in-Publication Data
A catalogue record for this book is available from the British Library

ISBN: 978-1-78240-585-6

This book was conceived, designed and produced by
Leaping Hare Press
58 West Street, Brighton BN1 2RA, United Kingdom

Creative Director PETER BRIDGEWATER
Publisher SOPHIE COLLINS
Commissioning Editor MONICA PERDONI
Art Director WAYNE BLADES
Senior Editor JAYNE ANSELL
Designer RICHARD CONSTABLE
Illustrators MELVYN EVANS, LYDIA CROOK

Printed in China

1 3 5 7 9 10 8 6 4 2

Contents

Introduction 6

Chapter One
Letting Go of Attachments 14

Chapter Two
Opening to Stillness & Solitude 48

Chapter Three
Meditation as Medicine for the Soul 86

Chapter Four
Embracing the Polarities in Life 120

Continuing the Journey 138

Acknowledgements 139
Bibliography 140
Resources 141
Index 142

INTRODUCTION

Mindfulness is a term that has gained increasing awareness in the minds of people in recent years. It's to do with dropping into yourself, becoming aware, finding a healthy balance between doing and being, becoming fully attentive to the present moment. Engaging fully in what 'is' (right now) rather than what 'should' or 'ought' to be. In the context of anger, allowing yourself to feel angry without reacting in any way, remaining open-hearted and empathetic — even though you want to strangle someone!

INTRODUCTION

BALANCE THROUGH MINDFULNESS

◆

By the time people embark on an anger management programme, their lives are so out of balance that anger is simply a manifestation of their state. In order to find balance we need to become mindful and through becoming mindful we create balance. We cannot have one without the other.

I HAVE BEEN HOLDING ANGER MANAGEMENT CLASSES at the British Association of Anger Management (BAAM) since 1990, and when I attended a Mindfulness Based Stress Reduction (MBSR) course in 2006, I discovered I was aligned to the practice and advocating its use to anger sufferers without even realizing it. In my workshops, I was already teaching skills in awareness – the key element of mindful anger management.

In my group sessions, I always illustrate the need for balance by recounting one of my favourite stories about Siddhartha (the Buddha's name before he became enlightened). As Siddhartha was crossing the River Ganges, his attention was caught by the way the water reeds were bending as the wind blew through them. He saw how the reeds that were too supple eventually became saturated and died, while the reeds that were too dry and brittle snapped or split and died. However, the reeds that were neither too supple nor too dry remained alive and continued to flourish. In that moment he began to develop his teachings on finding 'the middle path'.

INTRODUCTION

Finding the Middle Ground

The basic premise of mindfulness that I teach is to help people who suffer from anger to learn how to delay gratification and tolerate sitting in the discomfort of their feelings – especially anger! When eventually they're able to do that, they experience a new freedom – the freedom of finding the middle ground. Instead of exploding, they can contain their impulses and express themselves cleanly; or they can find a way to be assertive rather than bottling up and imploding. It is by understanding how our mind works that we can control our anger, and mindfulness is the key.

My Path to Anger Management

I came to this work through my own struggle with one of my biggest issues in life – I could not tolerate conflict and arguments. Today this would be termed 'conflict avoidant'. Despite my training as a counsellor I had no idea how to deal with conflict, anger or any other form of resolving disputes.

I began to realize that being angry and yet conflict avoidant was an effective way to avoid dealing with the depression I was suffering from. For years I didn't even realize I was depressed. I had no benchmark or yardstick for determining whether I was depressed or not – I just seemed to be in a perpetual state of confusion, felt isolated, misunderstood, alone and often overwhelmed. Finally, Fritz Perls' definition of depression being 'anger turned inwards' hit home – it struck a chord deep inside me, and I remember thinking that I couldn't be the only one who felt as furious as I did. There had to be others who felt like me at some point or another. How come people never talked about their feelings of anger? Why were we so disconnected from our anger, considering the challenges we are faced with on a daily basis?

From Avoidance to Expression
It took me years to fully grasp the complexity of how my anger ruled my life. From being the archetypal conflict avoidant and expressing myself passive-aggressively by using provocative comments, or sarcasm, or winding people up, I went to being the full-on, explosive, in-your-face angry man. I won't deny that I actually loved this new feeling of omnipotence. I had finally found my voice and boy, was I going to make sure everyone heard it. Of course it didn't work. If anything, it polarized me even more. My inability to self-regulate became my demise. Those who had loved and respected me became afraid of me and started to avoid me. Others just ended up not taking me seriously, which angered me more.

In the end, it was the wise words of my mentor that shifted my perception. He quietly suggested that maybe I needed to experience the two extremes of anger in order to discover where I could stand, and I realized that I did indeed need to live in the centre of these two polarities. I needed to find the balance. I had become so out of control that in order to find this balance I had to experience the full range of expression. To me, that was an incredible revelation and the next big step towards becoming mindful. The fundamental discovery I made was that when I found myself imploding, I needed to navigate towards finding the courage to stand up for myself. When I found myself exploding, I needed to use my mindfulness strategies to contain a potential outburst by reminding myself of the negative consequences. These two polarities became my beacon towards being mindfully vigilant, just in time to pull me back from the brink of emotional and verbal violence.

About This Book

This book has four sections exploring the art of mindfulness as a tool to liberate you from your anger before it progresses into the territory of violence:

- *Letting go of attachments*
- *Opening to stillness and solitude*
- *Meditation as a medicine*
- *Embracing the polarities in life.*

The task here is to help you get to grips with the source of your anger and how to control it, how mindfulness can help you to understand your feelings better, and what it means to live in the here and now.

INTRODUCTION

This book also aims to help you build a better infrastructure in which to control your anger, part of which will be to turn your unhealthy expression of anger into a healthy expression. You will learn that anger can be a gift and is best used to heal situations rather than to destroy everything that stands in its way. It can become your ally. To some that may seem like an impossible idea, but imagine what a different world it would be if people were able to use their anger for positive change – consider the achievements of Gandhi, Malcolm X and Nelson Mandela, for example.

Each section works towards building an understanding that in order to control your anger, you actually need to express it. This is a paradoxical truism and as much of a challenge for the individual who says too much too soon as it is for those who can't get the words out. Fundamentally, this book is an invitation to you to use your anger in a constructive and healthy way, and mindfulness will be your guiding light.

Changing the habit of a lifetime will take an enormous amount of effort and practice, but please remember – great cities were not built in a day.

'Your worst enemy cannot harm you as much as
your own unguarded thoughts.'

BUDDHA

JOURNAL WRITING

❖

'Journal writing is a voyage to the interior.'

FROM 'ONE TO ONE: SELF-UNDERSTANDING
THROUGH JOURNAL WRITING' BY CHRISTINA BALDWIN
M. EVANS & CO. INC., 1977, UPDATED 1991

❖

Keeping an anger journal is like having a bowl in which you place precious trinkets about yourself – you discover new insights you may never have observed before. If you don't already keep a journal, I recommend buying a notepad for jotting down your thoughts and feelings during reflective time.

WRITING IN A JOURNAL allows you to bear witness to your own behaviour and internal logic, as well as providing a way of identifying repetitive patterns you could easily ignore. If you tend to be angry, journal writing will help to stop the anger taking up space in your head. This is critical, because recording your thoughts and feelings in relation to your anger is not only cathartic, but also allows you to review your motivations or identify any future anger triggers. It is easy to lose sight of this information when you are caught up in the moment.

You'll find various journal exercises throughout this book to encourage time for expression and reflection. You can order a personalized journal from *www.angermindfulness.co.uk*.

CHAPTER ONE

LETTING GO OF ATTACHMENTS

We, as humans, need to evolve into accepting the basic fact of life that suffering follows the loss of transient things. There are many instances whereby we can monitor and regulate our emotional suffering by making mature choices through being mindful and aware of the consequences. Our challenge is to choose what we are willing to suffer for — and then to accept responsibility for the inconvenience of the suffering we have imposed upon ourselves.

> **Compassionate Detachment**
>
> 'Compassionate detachment simply means we are not attached physically, spiritually, mentally and especially emotionally to the events, things, and people in our lives that we have compassion for. This does not mean we don't care – because compassion is caring. It means we are not attached in a way that fails to serve the highest good of all.'
>
> RALPH P. BROWN
> MOHAWK ARTIST & INSTRUCTOR ON THE USE
> OF THE MEDICINE WHEEL

COMPASSIONATE DETACHMENT & EMPATHY

For those who are frequently short-tempered, the idea of exercising 'compassionate detachment and empathy' in a moment of outrage is like a red rag to a bull. When a person is furious, these qualities take a brief vacation. However, compassionate detachment and empathy are among the best antidotes to anger.

COMPASSIONATE DETACHMENT is synonymous with mindfulness. Mindfulness is being completely in tune with, and aware of, the present moment. It is also being committed to a non-evaluative and non-judgemental approach to your

own and another person's inner experience. For example, a mindful approach to one's inner experience is simply viewing 'thoughts as thoughts' as opposed to evaluating certain thoughts as positive or negative, good or bad, right or wrong, black or white. Adopting an attitude of empathy buys you time. Instead of creating a catastrophic result, you can approach a situation with a more open heart and mind, which allows for more solutions of mutual benefit to occur that may not have been considered before.

At first, the concept of combining anger with mindfulness appears to be an oxymoron. However, with some training and awareness, when we feel our anger being triggered we can also use it to serve as a white flag to switch into a more conscious state of being. In this way, being mindful becomes an interference to a potential outburst. Before our anger gets out of control we can bring all our awareness to the event and accept things the way they are. We can become empathetic to the other person. We can let go of our expectations and our attachment to winning or being right. We can connect to our breathing and remain calm. We can engage any other strategy that helps us to not fly off the handle and overreact. We can do everything we don't do, but need to do, when angry.

Mindfulness is being completely in tune with, and aware of, the present moment.

Imagine a Mindful World...

A mindful approach to life is about developing awareness of our own nature and expectations and then making healthy choices. It's a continual practice because life is in constant motion and therefore demands that we regularly assess, address and attend to every single detail. It beckons us to become aware of how our action or 'inaction' has an effect. The last thing someone in the throes of anger is aware of is their impact on the object of their abuse – whereas those who live with angry people tend to be overly cautious, desperately trying to minimize the effect or compensate for them. At a very fundamental level, living our lives mindfully could cure the ills of the world, but – like many things in life – it either comes naturally to us or has to be worked at. Either way, it is never static – we can only deepen into the perspective of

---

A High Price to Pay

Throughout my years of delivering anger management courses I have been witness to the turmoil and trauma an angry person experiences because they're so preoccupied in being 'right', 'taking the moral high ground' and ultimately 'winning' – whatever the cost to themselves or to others. I have found this heartbreaking, because often the price is just too damn high and the damage irreparable.

LETTING GO OF ATTACHMENTS

objectivity and become increasingly acute in our observations. Can you imagine the world if everyone put that much care and attention into their actions? There is much literature on this paradigm and it's most certainly taking more root in our world, with real benefits.

◆

'There has probably never been a time where there has been so much fear and conflict across the world, not just across oceans and borders but across the breakfast table. In fact many now prefer conflict to peace, as they become addicted to the actions of anger and aggression, and the adrenaline rush that results. They don't really want conflict to end, in fact, they will say that some conflict is good to get things done and stimulate change. They are not aware that they are killing themselves. All conflict is simply a symptom of attachment to a position. And as we know, this generates fear, and fear, if allowed to stay, eventually kills its host. All solutions are based on detachment or letting go. But that will be difficult until we can see that all possession is an illusion, that we have nothing to lose and that there are no victories in winning.'

BRAHMA KUMARIS WORLD SPIRITUAL UNIVERSITY, MT ABU, RAJASTHAN

◆

THE TWO FACES OF ANGER

We all encounter the many faces of anger in our lives, but they are displayed primarily in two ways. Passive-aggressive anger represents the role of the imploder, often described as 'cold' anger, while aggressive anger represents the role of the exploder, or 'hot' anger.

REGARDLESS OF WHETHER you are an imploder or exploder – and many of us have both aspects – unchecked anger is harmful to your health and to others around you. We will look at this in more detail later in the book; for the moment, though, let's explore how anger reveals itself.

Passive-Aggressive Anger

Passive-aggressive anger starts out as implosive, but will eventually become explosive. A person who does not express their anger, holding in the resentment or fury they feel (often for hours, days, weeks, months or even years), is like a pot simmering on the stove – at some point it will reach boiling point and bubble over. Depending on how tight that pot's lid is, things can reach a point where the internal pressure is simply too great and a big eruption is inevitable. Perhaps disappointingly, internalizing anger can be far unhealthier than constantly expressing it, as an exploder would do. One would wish to be rewarded for being so restrained – but unfortunately it just doesn't work like that.

Suppressed Feelings

The danger of unexpressed anger is that it can turn even further inwards and become a form of depression. One could almost say the stronger the suppression, the deeper the depression. We also need to remember that an imploder is not only suppressing anger – there can also be fear, hurt, shame and sadness, and the imploder will be just as uncomfortable with these feelings as with the anger itself.

Why suppress these feelings, you may ask? The reasons are very complex and individual, but are usually the end result of received messages suggesting that expressing our feelings was inappropriate. Showing any emotional vulnerability was a sign of weakness and made us open to attack and ridicule. I've heard many examples in my workshops of messages received in childhood, but the one that stands out the most is: 'Anger is dangerous and threatening.' In some instances this is quite literal and true. Of course if anger is 'dangerous and threatening' it has to be suppressed, no matter what the emotional cost. Anger becomes the enemy and has to be suppressed in order to survive. Do you recognize this type of behaviour in yourself or others? Do you suffer from depression?

Aggressive Anger

In polarity to the passive-aggressive types, the individuals displaying aggressive behaviour are explosive, trigger-happy and volcanic in nature. Exploders find it virtually impossible to

> **'I Never Get Angry'**
>
> Being an anger management guru, I hear a lot of amusing (to me, anyway!) comments from people at social events, and one of the most common is: 'I never get angry.' Sometimes people take great pride in this – they perceive not getting angry as a reflection of their ability to control their feelings. (Invariably this statement is followed by them saying that they know someone who is angry!) These types are masters at repressing most of their feelings, including anger. It takes a lot of vital energy to do this and when they do explode it's terrifying for others, who have become accustomed to their cool, calm exterior.

contain their anger. They fly off the handle at the slightest threat to their fragile ego or personal safety. I describe these types of people as throwing 'angrenades' as part of their emotional arsenal. Exploders will always tell you what is going on for them in no uncertain terms – they don't beat around the bush and often go for the jugular instantly. They are constantly on red alert and react to situations without ever thinking the situation through, never mind considering the consequences of their actions. However, the positive side to this behaviour is that you always know where you stand with them – because they tell you so! This is in stark contrast to imploders, who

tend to be more devious and surreptitious — and by the time you find out they're angry with you, it's too late to do anything about it.

Containing Explosive Anger

I often hear exploders saying things like, 'I cannot contain my anger.' However, this is not quite true. There are many situations where they have no choice *but* to contain their anger and frustration, because if they didn't they would be faced with dire consequences — for example, losing the deal when negotiating with a challenging customer or client, or possibly losing their livelihoods if they speak disrespectfully to the boss or other staff members, or even when in conflict with a traffic warden or having to pull themselves together before acting out in a public place. Can you recall some of the consequences you have already had to deal with when you've completely lost it? Make a note of them in your journal.

> *I often hear exploders say, 'I cannot contain my anger.' However, this is not quite true. There are many situations where they have no choice but to.*

So it is entirely possible for exploders to contain their rogue feelings and it's usually in situations where they might not have any real power or authority. These are situations where they often feel psychologically impotent. By exploding,

they could compromise their circumstances severely – but as we all know, sometimes their anger still gets the better of them. This can leave them with feelings of guilt and remorse.

What's Your Style?

Now that you have a sense of the way anger is expressed, make a note in your journal of which style is more relevant to you. You may well experience being an imploder at home, but an exploder while you are driving your car. If so, make a note of both indications.

Exploders & Mindfulness

Where mindfulness is concerned, you could easily argue that exploders don't have a clue as to what it means to be aware. They have little understanding of the impact their anger has on people around them. The concept of being introspective or reflective before getting to the point of explosion is simply not in their emotional vocabulary.

But being mindful is a discipline that can be learnt and, once put into practice, allows you to bring awareness to the situation and stop the anger from spilling over. You might end up simmering, but at least the inappropriate behaviour is contained. In this way you will spare yourself, as well as those closest to you, the fallout of your fury.

Surviving Anger

◆

Survivors of other people's anger develop an acute sense of anticipating the behaviour of their partner, child, boss or parent in a constant effort to avoid conflict. They train themselves to be sensitized to when an angry outburst is imminent and are generally masters at this skill.

Survivors also seem to have the knack of defusing anger. Obviously this is not always the case, but often when a hothead is about to blow up, the survivor has put in place a strategy that minimizes the escalation. One of the most effective strategies I've heard time and again from survivors is simply to listen – interestingly, a skill that a hothead is the least effective at and needs to master.

Hotheads generally lack the emotional wherewithal to detach themselves from a potentially volatile situation, never mind consider being empathetic towards their target. They

---

Definition of Survivors

People who I call 'survivors' are those at the receiving end of others' mental and verbal abuse, who have had to train themselves, often since childhood, to be mindful of containing their thoughts and feelings in order to keep out of danger's way.

often take everything too personally and in that moment they want to exterminate the person who has undermined them. As we have already seen, they tend to exhibit a neurotic impulse to be 'right' or to 'win' in any social engagement. Being right or winning affirms their sense of self and self-worth (ego identity) – therefore, what they perceive as an attack on their self-worth is worth going to war over. They lack the patience or emotional skill-set to contain any overwhelming and intense rogue feelings that may be triggered, such as shame, fear and anger. In this state there is absolutely no awareness of the language they're using or how their anger is impacting on those around them. Their only motivation is an ego attachment to stay on top of the situation and maintain the moral high ground.

Hotheads hold this position as fiercely as a bulldog that is unwilling to let go of a stick and would rather die before admitting defeat. Consequences at this stage become irrelevant and they don't care who is caught in the crossfire of their egocentric determination. Compassion and empathy have left the building, only to return in remorse when the hothead steps back into the wake of the damage done.

Conversely, imploders never allow their frustrations to be externalized or expressed. They have trained themselves to freeze people out because of their fear of being rejected and abandoned, the result of when they first began to express their anger within the family system or elsewhere.

Resistance to Feeling Our Feelings

The reason we tend to implode or explode is because of our attachment to *not* feeling strong feelings. We have resistance to feeling fear, hurt, shame and sadness. These are very powerful feelings, so it's easy to be overwhelmed by them – but it's also entirely possible to engage with them in a way that establishes a sense of well-being. It takes some emotional resilience, but mostly it's about actually giving yourself permission to feel all your feelings and to accept the way things are. This in itself is a step towards becoming mindful. It's a position of being more compassionate and empathetic towards yourself and, in turn, others around you.

WHAT DRIVES OUR ATTACHMENTS?

Living in a post-modern contemporary society contributes inextricably to our obsessions – our neurotic drives. We are addicted to instant gratification, to being happy and successful and to any 'quick fix' that will get us there. We are even more preoccupied and consumed with how our world sees us.

PROFILE PAGES, SOCIAL MEDIA, ONLINE MARKETING and networking platforms demand that we stay on top of our game, keep up with the hottest trends and constantly update ourselves – they're the modern-day vanity board. It's an endless pursuit of perfecting our ego identity. We invest an enormous amount of time and energy into an ideal projected image of ourselves and we believe it to be true, even though it is inauthentic. We become attached to this image because we don't want people to see who we really are – our faults and failings, our real sense of inferiority, our insecurities and imperfections. We want never to have to expose our deepest fears, truths and longings. We are so attached to being seen in this perfected way by our peers that any threat to this image is deemed intolerable by the ego – the mechanism that drives our attachments.

> *Most angry people have no idea who they are, what they believe in or what they stand for.*

Living in a world obsessed with perfection – be that physical, emotional, mental, even spiritual – only adds to the fact that when anything threatens their ego, people get angry. The more we really believe that our created image of ourselves is the whole reflection of who we are, the quicker we are to use anger to protect what is perceived as an assault. Aggression is an especially effective weapon to use against those threatening our invested identity. The irony here is that most angry people have no idea who they are, what they believe in or what they stand for – and they certainly wouldn't have a clue as to what it means to have meaning in their lives.

The Fight-or-Flight Response

On top of this (and to their disadvantage), when people feel even the slightest bit threatened, an ancient and automatic central nervous system defence mechanism kicks in. Unfortunately, this actually reduces their options to a primal imperative – they can fight the threat, flee from it or, failing that, shut down and freeze from it. Our brains, being geared up to be energy efficient, perceive these options as an instant solution – although it is not the best solution.

The part of the brain known as the 'old' brain – which represents the limbic system, controlling our basic emotions and drives – does not have the wherewithal to differentiate between the past, present or future. This is its neurological prerogative. Despite what you may think is going on in your head, the body and central nervous system experience any kind of threat as a danger to life and hence will activate whatever is necessary for survival. It's designed to keep you safe. At the point that the old brain registers something amiss, it kick-starts into action – your heart rate and pulse increase, your palms begin to sweat, and you become increasingly angry in defence. Adrenaline and cortisol pump through your veins and your whole biology and psychology prepare for war.

What we need to get to grips with is that there is in fact no threat as such, only the illusion of a threat. The old brain is susceptible to pain and pleasure and does not have the capacity to discern. Its sole purpose is to keep us alive. The old brain is not hard-wired to detach and, by trying its best to protect us, it actually gets us into hot water and causes a lot of mayhem. It's the new brain – the neocortex – that has the capacity to understand, make sense of challenging situations, rationalize, think linearly and laterally and reframe experiences. By so doing, the new brain allows us to self-regulate and not become overwhelmed by old-brain stimuli. The new brain becomes our best friend in these situations.

The Domain of Mindfulness

The real danger in anger is the fact that we misinterpret situations because we haven't created enough time and space to consider the reality of the situation and whether or not we're in any danger. It is entirely possible to train the brain to manage what is seen as a potential threat – and mindfulness goes a long way towards this.

Once we realize the limitations of the old brain and how it hijacks our bodies, we can begin to deploy the new brain to do its job of regulating and moderating our natural impulses and instincts. The new brain is the domain of mindfulness; it has the capacity to reflect, to be introspective, calm and thoughtful. If we don't train ourselves to be mindful, we will keep overreacting to situations, caught in the constant trap of our own sabotage. This behaviour keeps us stuck in outdated and damaging internal thought processes. It reinforces our hostility and, by default, the pain and suffering for everyone.

Engaging the New Brain

Learning to be mindful is to allow ourselves to feel our feelings, monitor our automatic responses, employ strategies to regulate them and consider our options. Mindfulness is about creating a space (internally or externally) so we can gain objectivity and come up with more effective solutions. It allows us to pull back from a situation and not get caught up in those attachments of looking good, being right, winning or being in control. It does take skill and practice – but there is a lot more to gain from it than being continuously hijacked by the old brain.

The new brain opens up a world of creative solutions for dealing with emotional distress. It facilitates our ability to be logical, reasonable, rational; it aids communication. It opens us to new ideas and new ways of thinking and has the capacity to understand and make sense of why we feel what we feel, why we do what we do, and why it's imperative to make fundamental changes in our lives in order to grow emotionally.

> *Mindfulness is about creating a space so we can gain objectivity and come up with more effective solutions.*

A Mindfulness Meditation

This simple mindfulness meditation is designed to engage the new brain, opening to the present and new possibilities in cultivating discipline. It can be downloaded from *www.angermindfulness.co.uk*.

Find a comfortable place where you can sit and be undisturbed. Begin to observe your environment in every detail. When you feel you have fully taken in your environment, bring your awareness to your breathing. Follow your breath in and out of your body. Simply follow the gentle rising and sinking of your chest, how it expands and where your breath moves to; do not force anything. Just allow the natural motion to occur and observe how it changes. You may notice that as soon as you place your attention on your breath for even a few moments, it will respond by slowing down. Enjoy those deeper breaths.

Next, notice your body posture – how is your body taking up the space around you? What is it in contact with? Are there any aches and pains? Where are you holding tension? Give these areas some attention and breathe into them. Notice if this helps to relax the areas or if there is any change. Try not to move too quickly. Allow your body to guide you.

Now close your eyes. This allows you to focus internally more clearly. Again, allow there to be a soft focus on your breathing. See if you can hold only your in-breath and out-breath in your attention. When you feel more settled, see if you can breathe in for the count of seven and out for the count of seven. Try not to force anything. If you can't reach seven, that's fine. The idea is simply to lengthen each breath. Greet each breath with acceptance and continue until you find an easy, deep rhythm.

Once you feel very comfortable with that, see if you can really focus your attention on the air entering your nostrils, travelling down into your lungs. Simply explore if you can follow its path. In and back out again – this substance entering your body. Notice where your body wants to move it and allow your sensations to guide you. Be curious and playful.

If your mind wanders, just gently bring it back to your in- and out-breath. There may be racing thoughts or even mild irritation at the task – and that's ok. Notice the internal chatter, distractions or even judgements. Accept their arising and continue with the task.

Ideally spend ten minutes practising this meditation. When you feel a sense of relaxation or just feel more settled in your body, gently open your eyes. Give yourself a few moments to adjust to being back in the room. Any change in your metabolism is great. The more you practise this meditation, the deeper states of being you will achieve. If you found it difficult and became impatient, that's also ok. Simply notice where you started and ended up, and record this in your journal. Be diligent and you will soon notice a difference in your experience every time.

This meditation is the beginning of taming the wild horses or drunken monkeys in your head. It's about not letting them rule your life, giving them (quite literally) some breathing space and including an awareness of your body. It's about having an encounter with the present, developing a relationship to this, and using your breath as a tool. This is something you can do whenever you choose, wherever you are. You have all the tools necessary. It simply needs a decision to take time out. We suggest at least once a day – but don't be surprised to find yourself wanting to do more!

What it Means to be Present

◆

'The living moment is everything.'

D.H. LAWRENCE
ENGLISH NOVELIST, POET & PLAYWRIGHT

◆

Living a mindful life and bringing our attention to the present moment is difficult to achieve in our busy schedules. We are so constantly torn by our work, family and social demands that giving up time to attend to 'nothing' seems ludicrous.

When I first read the D.H. Lawrence quote above I was struck by its simplicity. Had I read this 25 years ago it would have passed me by. I was far too disassociated ever to consider the truth of it. I was bouncing between the past and the future like a ping-pong ball, doing my best to get through a day as uneventfully as possible. Becoming present would have required me to slow down and experience the

> 'Having spent the better part of my life trying either to relive the past or experience the future before it arrives, I have come to believe that in between these two extremes is peace.'
>
> ANON

living moment. That's what I like most about this quote. Back then, being with myself was too painful and I would have been unavailable to the living moment around me. Now I am able to appreciate that there *is only* this moment and it is alive, pulsing, connected and…everything.

BEING PRESENT

Let's consider what being present means for you. Record your discoveries in your journal.

- *What is your experience of the here and now and what does it mean to you?*
- *Are you aware of when you are in the past, present or future? How do you know this?*
- *Have you ever thought about the importance of being in the moment?*

The Power of Now

In his best-selling book *The Power of Now*, Eckhart Tolle suggests that we don't have to stop being busy, stop doing things, but we can intersperse our lives with brief moments of presence. For example, right now you can become alert, aware of your surroundings, of your sense perceptions. At this moment, allow everything to be as it is. Then become aware that there

is an awareness here, a consciousness, and that *that* is more truly who you are than anything else. I like this suggestion – that being present is not another task to complete. This is something you can 'intersperse' in your daily schedules. You don't need a particular place or tool, just you, right now, right here – shifting your attention from all that doing to simply being and sensing.

Freedom in a Thought

Becoming mindful is about consciously choosing what we will let in and what we will shut out. It's about developing the skill to control the noise in our heads and lives; learning to listen to our bodies, to trust our senses and respect them. Making a conscious decision about what you will engage in not only applies to the world out there, but also to your internal world. Real freedom is when you get to the point in your life where you can choose how much time you're prepared to let a feeling – anger, or any other debilitating one – rent space in your head. This is not about ignoring our feelings or denying their relevance. It's about how to acknowledge what is, remain compassionately detached and still be open. It's a supreme way of self-management. It takes skill and practice and it helps to recognize that, at a very deep level, all things are impermanent. You don't have to be attached to one outcome. Everything changes and it's ok. There is no judgement on what occurs, it just occurs. There can be tremendous freedom in a thought.

LETTING GO OF ATTACHMENTS

A Malign Influence?

Our culture is driven by commerce, to profit by consumerism. Advertising, the media's very convincing messenger, uses sophisticated and expensive strategies, costing trillions annually, to influence our thinking, feelings and definition of reality. Let's explore the media's influence on our lives.

The media can influence you to live in the past, convince you to feel better about yourself right now, or get you to fantasize about the future. It surreptitiously drives you to yearn for the things you don't have and, more importantly, don't even need. Even more astonishing is that what was once mostly about selling product is now a culture selling information. We've been conned into believing that information is power and, if you want to be powerful, you must stay informed. Being tuned in gets the popularity vote more than being tuned out. This is extended into our 'online status' – the more activity you create, the more friends you're likely to have. You just can't get away from being constantly plugged in and the accessibility of digital technology is designed to keep it that way.

The Temptations of Marketing

Marketing companies know exactly how to tap into what makes us feel good. If, for example, you had an amazing

childhood in a particular era and you loved the way your life was, you will be influenced by nostalgia – and you will be drawn to buying products and services designed with a very nostalgic 'feel'. Similarly, if you're a futurist and love being the first to have all the new technologies and you're a sucker for the latest fads – well, you'll be hooked right into all the hottest gadgets targeting people just like you! Whether you're a label addict or a lifestyle junkie, there's something for everyone.

I am not suggesting we have to live our lives as puritans. What I am proposing is that we could be more mindful of how our lives are influenced by a highly sophisticated system designed to make us feel better about ourselves by compulsively selling us stuff we could comfortably live without. It's fundamental that we look at what our priorities are.

What We Own Is Not Who We Are
There's nothing wrong in enjoying buying a new product or owning the latest gadget. I am the first to accept this – but I'm also aware that what I own is not a reflection of my true nature. A product is not going to make me feel any better about myself, it's not going to increase my self-esteem and it's most certainly not going to make me feel like a million dollars – even if that's what it cost. It's useful having clarity about what really makes you happy – what motivates you, inspires you and touches you emotionally.

Some of my clients who come to see me aged 30 to 50 cannot believe they need to visit an anger management guru. But it's easy to see why they're so angry. They figured they had their lives sorted. According to their checklist they have the trophy wife or husband and the three degrees. They have the perfect nuclear family, drive the coolest car and have access to the latest fads, not to mention the country house or the pad in some exotic hideaway. This is not an exaggeration. How can they be so peeved when they have it all? – and they're angry about that too! They've ticked all the boxes, yet feel gnawingly unfulfilled. It's tragic, very real and unbelievably frustrating.

Worshipping the Wrong God
What I became increasingly aware of in relation to this client group is that, for so many, their lives have no meaning – they followed the wrong god home. I don't mean 'god' in the religious or even spiritual sense, but in that they have made their desires and attachments their god and they've been completely hoodwinked by ownership, status and materialism.

They were trained to believe that having possessions, status, influence and power would be their elixir of life – but 'meaning' is not something you can buy off the shelf. In my experience with this particular client group, their lack of humility prevents them from experiencing meaning in their lives. This type of angry person can be highly opinionated, arrogant with a self-serving skewed morality, have a distorted value system and an unethical framework. They've used anger as well as these mechanisms to propel them up the 'success ladder', and it's only a matter of time until something gives. It can be the loss of a huge amount of money, career, position, wife, child, or just an intense sense of dissatisfaction or a feeling of losing control that brings them to sit in my office.

That Was Me...

I can say this because I am talking about myself. I know this terrain very well. I too fell into the same trap. I was very successful in my career at the early age of 27, I had all the money in the world, status, prestige, 'toys', the lifestyle – but I had no idea who I was. I was unbearably unhappy and seriously depressed and it was impossible for me to reconcile my depression because I had it all! I had everything money could buy, but nothing that it couldn't – meaning humility or happiness. No amount of pleasurable indulgences took my pain away and the more dissatisfied I was, the more angry I became.

At the point when I could tolerate my internal discomfort no longer and chose to set myself upon a different path, I decided to explore meditation at the suggestion of some good friends. From the ages of 28 to 34 I meditated religiously every single day for at least 30–60 minutes. I devoured books on comparative religion, and Buddhism became my road map. The idea of detachment became my god. I can see now how that served me – but it took me years to find out.

What I didn't quite realize is that unfortunately there were times when I was using meditation and Buddhist philosophy as yet another way to escape from myself, to stuff my feelings and – yes, you've got it – to avoid confronting my emotional pain and suffering.

I recognize now that at the time, when I read about detachment, I unconsciously chose not to read about compassionate detachment. Detaching without compassion makes for a very dangerous cocktail of denial and egocentric behaviour. I became a master of not feeling anything. Add cannabis to the mix and you have an emotional zombie.

There where times when meditation helped, but by and large it became a panacea for all my psychological ills. I wasn't the only one in this position – most of my friends and associates were doing the same thing, and we were all trying to find a quick fix and a way out of a very confusing emotional labyrinth of our own making and demise.

EXPLORING MEANING

Make a list of the things that give your life meaning.

If you cannot think of at least 20 things that give your life meaning, do some research – ask people what gives *their* life meaning and see if you can relate. You might surprise yourself.

SUFFERING IS AN OPTION & HAPPINESS IS A CHOICE

◆

In our own personal worlds we often encounter great emotional suffering. What we tend not to recognize is that we bring most of our suffering upon ourselves because we lack the emotional intelligence to navigate our inner turmoil.

IT IS EASY TO OVERLOOK THE FACT that angry people are actually suffering profoundly. We get so caught up in the horror of the passive-aggressive innuendos or aggressive barrage that of course our first impulse is to protect ourselves and choose not to engage them. This is understandable, and sometimes necessary. I have never met anyone with a severe anger problem who was not in profound emotional pain.

Almost 20 years ago I came across a revolutionary idea stating that happiness is a choice. Initially, this did not sit well with me. I was perplexed as to how happiness could be a choice. To me, happiness was a random fleeting experience, something you were lucky to feel in the moment (or not). I had spent so many years being unhappy that this thought really bugged me. My problem with the concept was that if one could choose to be happy, then one could also choose sadness, hurt, fear, shame or anger. The possibility intrigued me, but at the time I was too depressed to take it on board. I didn't feel I had a choice about anything and this concept just felt too abstract.

It's much easier for me today to embrace this concept. Years of personal development, therapy and training have enabled me not to be hijacked by my feelings. However, despite all this work, I now believe that the simple concept of having a choice as to how much energy I'm willing to invest in a feeling at any given moment is profoundly liberating.

Sound Investments

Taking responsibility for our decisions requires an ability to step back and be objective. If our anger is being triggered, we first need to accept responsibility for that fact and then give ourselves the chance to decide how much we want to invest in it.

It's convenient to believe that other people make us angry. The number of times I have heard how someone else was responsible for making someone feel something they didn't want to feel! It's simply not true – it's impossible. Only *you* can make you feel what you feel. There is no other you but you inside your head. Sure, others can emotionally manipulate us, but we still have the choice as to how much we will engage.

So if we can be our own masters and decide how much we will invest into any state of feeling, then happiness can become a choice. I do realize this is a difficult concept to accept and understand, never mind utilize. Some people may not even have access to the full range of their feelings yet. Angry people in particular suffer from the affliction of disassociating from their feelings and tend to default into anger. However, perhaps

it's useful to hold it in your awareness that you don't have to fall victim to your own rage, that you can exercise choice and begin to move towards that goal.

Developing an Emotional Language

If you feel faced with an impossible task, let this not discourage you. The first part of your journey is to develop a healthy, imaginative relationship to all your feelings – what I like to refer to as the full democracy of feelings. Keep reminding yourself to give permission to be sad, scared, hurt, powerful, ashamed, happy, peaceful and angry. It may feel overwhelming, but try to monitor it and be measured about your approach. If you feel severely handicapped, working with a professional counsellor or engaging in any personal development work might help.

The task is to understand your interior world of feelings and emotions and develop an emotional language. This is uniquely you, so give yourself time. It has taken every day of your life for you to get to where you are. If you feel too resistant or afraid of what you might encounter, remind yourself that it's precisely your unacknowledged feelings that are hijacking your life. Better to befriend them than to suppress them. In this way, you will have control of your feelings instead of allowing them to take you hostage and, in time, you will be even more able to exercise choice as to how long you are willing to be swamped by a feeling.

The Mechanism of Suffering

A lot of energy is used to suppress what you don't want to feel. Angry people are especially at the mercy of unexpressed feelings. Open them up to the full range of their feelings and their internal landscape changes – and so does their world view. They are no longer victims of their own suffering. This is an empowering and transformative place.

Let's look at how this feeds into the mechanism of suffering. Suffering is an emotion, a state you're in, not a feeling – unless it's physical. Deconstruct the emotional pain and you will discover a range of feelings that is driving the suffering. These may be a mixture of anger, sadness, hurt, fear or shame – the bag of feelings you don't like about yourself. The more you repress these feelings, the more pain you will have to endure and the more suffering you're inadvertently creating for yourself. This is paradoxical. You repress your feelings in an attempt to avoid pain, yet by so doing you create more pain and suffering.

Numbing the Senses
Suffering is often the result of years of suppressing your feelings. You may be completely unaware that you're in a state of suffering if all you feel is numb. However, this would mean that you're not able to feel fully happy either. In fact, from this position 'happy' is identified with how good you are at anaesthetizing yourself – how drunk you get, how many drugs you

can consume and any number of addictive behaviours that obliterate the senses. You have to ask yourself: 'If numbing yourself is worth it?'

The more avoidant you are of your feelings, the more your behaviour will be dysfunctional. When you drown yourself in all sorts of activities that keep you away from yourself, soon you won't be able to recognize who you really are. The more this happens – the further away you stray from your authentic self – the more angry you are likely to feel. While anger may be your method of defusing your internal pressure, it's also telling you something is very wrong. Something is amiss. This is when you can use your anger to become your ally and discover the truth behind it. Once you have developed a clear emotional narrative and have an understanding of your interior life, you allow others permission to do the same.

Addiction to Suffering

It might be worthwhile remembering that if you're caught in a negative cycle of consistently creating your suffering, you also have the ability – through choice – to uncreate it. Sometimes it's useful to reflect upon these things in a different way. You could also ask yourself the question: 'If I were to be without my suffering, where would that leave me?'

I have come across numerous instances where people are addicted to their suffering. If, for example, we're in a relationship with a person who contributes to our suffering, we have the choice to leave the relationship. We have the choice to end the suffering, or not. This might seem harsh and lacking in sight, but acknowledging the pain you're in takes courage; it also allows you to make some fundamental decisions about your life. I by no means underestimate how arduous a task it is to take action to end suffering, but people usually find that their suffering loses its sting as soon as they start to embrace and take responsibility for it.

INVESTIGATING YOUR SUFFERING

This is a challenging subject and it would be useful to spend time writing in your journal all the things you feel in relation to this concept. Perhaps you can start with a simple list of what you feel you are suffering for? Maybe even find the courage to speak to family and friends. Get some feedback from people you trust and whom you feel know you best. Please listen to the feedback without getting defensive or argumentative. That will defeat the purpose of this investigation, so keep an open mind.

In time, review your list and decide what you're willing to suffer for and what you're not. Then write a game plan for reducing this suffering. Simply reading this book may have given you choices you never thought of before.

CHAPTER TWO

OPENING TO STILLNESS & SOLITUDE

Stillness is anathema to our Western civilization. We live in a world whereby the more activity we're involved in, the more hip and cool we look and feel. However, the truth is more likely to be that no matter how much we do or are involved in, it will not change the way we perceive ourselves. We simply pay a massive price for our busyness, which is evident in how stressed we are, how exhausted, fatigued and — in more extreme cases — ill. Opening to stillness and solitude is a step towards overcoming this undesirable state.

Befriending Stillness

Taking time out of our pursuit of 'doing' allows space for the soul to deepen and breathe. The pathway to experiencing tranquillity is to befriend stillness and solitude, which allows you to perceive and relate differently to your world.

MANY PEOPLE SIMPLY ACCEPT that stress is part of life, but few of us have an acute sense of what it's actually doing to our bodies. We tend not to relate to our central nervous system as such — we simply take it for granted that it functions in the background, maintaining our homeostasis, and that there are times when we feel wired and others when we do not. But our bodies serve as an invaluable barometer for when things are running out of control. Angry people are often very out of touch with their systems, but fall victim to its surges of adrenaline (the 'red mist' phenomenon is a good example). Sometimes their problem lies not in the anger itself but in the lack of acknowledgement as to how saturated they feel — how stressed out they are.

I don't believe I have ever worked with an individual who has issues with anger who does not at the same time have a reduced ability to cope with life. Angry people do not manage their stress levels because they don't even recognize they're stressed. The reason their anger keeps tripping them up is that they are under-resourced to deal with life's challenges.

If we could have a more constant relationship with our bodies, we would pick up signals long before stress gets out of control. This would prevent an enormous amount of stress, anxiety and uncontrolled anger in our lives. Learning to de-stress and relax enables us to reduce our angry reactions by at least 30 per cent, if not more.

A Yearning for Silence

Exercise brings a certain relief from stress but, again, it's achieved through action. Much deeper states of stillness and relaxation are experienced by those who choose to pursue avenues that involve listening to the body and practising conscious awareness – yoga, tai chi, chi kung to name a few.

Another possibility is to consider a silent retreat or one of the body therapies that engage stillness as part of their modality, such as craniosacral therapy or Bowen technique. Engaging in these modalities opens up awareness of the health of our systems and it therefore becomes easier to monitor when imbalance is occurring, allowing us to take the necessary steps to rectify the situation.

If none of these options interest you, then engage in activities where you can enjoy calmness in your own company – long walks, cycling, fishing, any craft or artistic pursuit. Essentially you want to give yourself a breather from the world, a moment in time when you are not answerable to anyone and you can discover and enjoy your own space.

Stillness in itself is a rich and nourishing force. The soul yearns for silence. When we have a relationship with stillness and silence, it's not experienced as empty and boring, but as full, potent and resourcing. In this space, we're not switched off or shut down from life, but actually fully engaged with the source of life at a deep, primal and visceral level. The experience of being engaged with stillness in a conscious way will always be deeply personal and profound.

'There is no need to go to India or anywhere else to find peace. You will find that deep place of silence right in your room, your garden or even your bathtub.'

ELISABETH KÜBLER-ROSS
SWISS-BORN PSYCHIATRIST & AUTHOR

Help is at Hand

Fortunately, we live in a world where we have access to so many paradigms that can help with tuning in to ourselves. We all have our limitations, and sometimes discovering what they are is the key. Pushing yourself beyond your vitality doesn't serve you, or anyone around you.

If, on the other hand, you're suffering from post-traumatic stress disorder, you have been severely compromised on a fundamental level and you will need to address releasing and integrating the trauma before considering anything else. There is a vast amount of information available on this subject.

Whatever the source of your stress, it's useful to remember that there are many methodologies available that can really help. When you are in a healthy, resourced place, it's amazing what you can tackle without feeling overwhelmed. In fact, challenges are a joy – not because you are driven to prove yourself, but because you have the health, strength and focus to meet anything you choose.

The Principles of Anger Management

There are two fundamental principles of anger management. One is to listen, and the other is to stop, think and take a look at the bigger picture. Both are indicators to step back and be objective, and serve to remind us that silence and solitude are key to managing anger.

WE TEACH THESE PRINCIPLES in our anger management courses. Understanding written theory is easy for those who can cognitively grasp the ideas – the challenge is to apply the theory to your life and put it into practice, to have an encounter with the work. This is the main reason we refer to our courses as 'experiential'. The interaction between course participants triggers a whole new aspect; witnessing others in a similar position and gaining their support is deeply affirming and helps to integrate the theory into everyday life. People offer new ways of thinking you may never have considered. Despite only spending 30 hours or three days being focused and engaged with your personal history and your struggle to manage your intense feelings, there's something incredibly reassuring to know you're not the only one in this boat – and in fact you find you also have wisdoms to offer. A programme creates a structure for you to take into the world and apply. There's no doubt that adding stillness and solitude to your practice outside the group experience helps enormously to promote a healthier relationship with your anger.

The Challenge of Relaxing

I remember doing an assessment with a very angry young woman, and I asked her if she ever relaxed. She felt she did, and her partner nodded in agreement; but when I asked if that included switching off her brain, she seemed confused and perplexed as to why she would want to do that. I believe this reflects most people's understanding of relaxing – it's about being physically inactive. However, they overlook that while the body is inactive the brain is still racing at a million miles per hour, so they are never truly 'switched off'.

Almost all the exploders I have ever worked with have absolutely no relationship with relaxation. They are usually highly strung, hot-wired and short-tempered. They get annoyed when you suggest they could chill out, and have zero tolerance for what they see as doing nothing. Obviously there is a correlation between this and their anger.

I completely identify with this position and constantly have to monitor my own urges to steam ahead. This has been one of my biggest hurdles to overcome. A constantly overactive central nervous system meant that slowing down and becoming still was more like an existential death to me than an opportunity to relax. Every time I tried, I judged myself as being too lazy, which then kick-started me straight back into 'doing' mode.

Creating Time to Relax

Here is a list of activities that you can consider doing in order to help you relax:

- *Taking a hot bath or shower*
- *Deep breathing*
- *Listening to relaxing music*
- *Stretching exercises*
- *Having a massage*
- *Engaging in a craft activity*
- *Reading books that inspire you*
- *Baking a cake or kneading bread*
- *Going to the gym or exercising*
- *Completing a puzzle, jigsaw, sudoku*
- *Taking a nap*
- *Drawing or painting*
- *Writing in your journal*
- *Walking or cycling*
- *Visiting the seaside*
- *Knitting*
- *Meditating*

Arriving at Stillness

I have trained myself to relax by exploring different approaches that prompt me to slow down and become still. The first step that works best for me is to engage in a creative process – drawing, photography or sculpture. It's the one method that takes me out of my head and places me in a different mode of being. Focusing on just one activity brings me right into the present. I actually notice myself feeling calmer and more relaxed because I'm doing something I love. From this place I shift naturally into stillness and silence, and I can then decide whether I want to continue being still, or relax or even drift off to sleep. Sometimes I arrive at stillness by listening to chill-out music and move from there into silence; or I make a point of setting aside time to meditate.

Meditation APPS

A lovely meditation APP is available for the iPhone, called Zazen. You select the length of meditation you want to do, set the timer, and an assortment of bells indicates certain intervals and reminds you when you're coming to the end. You will also find apps on *www.angermindfulness.co.uk*. I encourage you to find methods of meditation that work for you. Ultimately, the longer the meditation is, the better off you will be.

OPENING TO STILLNESS & SOLITUDE

JOURNAL TASK

If you find it difficult to accept the concept of stillness or to practise mindfulness meditation, a good place to start is to engage in an artistic process or physical exercise. The idea is to get your brain to switch off and your body to de-stress. Take your journal and, in some quiet time, reflect on a few of the things you've done in the past that brought you joy and helped you relax. If you need to be reminded, ask family members or revisit a previous passion and re-engage with it. Record your findings in your journal.

The aim is to get used to the idea of being unstimulated, to engage in activities that leave you feeling peaceful as opposed to adrenalized. Even if it's only for 15 minutes a day, it's a beginning, and you can work at increasing it. Notice what effect it has on your well-being and outlook to life, and record those feelings in your journal also.

One Step at a Time

For those of you who are not already practising meditation, I want you to begin to learn what it means to relax properly so that moving into a practice of meditation – of engaging stillness and solitude – is something that feels less frightening.

It's important to become familiar with what it means to slow down your internal experiences so that you no longer overreact to situations. When you start to understand the mechanics of your body – to recognize when it's deeply relaxed and when you're fired up – you begin to know when you're in the right frame of mind to make a decision, and when you're not. In this way, your body becomes an extremely accessible barometer to manage the curve balls life throws.

Consider what happens when you return from a holiday. Have you noticed how for the first 72 hours you're still fairly relaxed and can cope with more challenges than you're used to? After that, you start resorting to your old habits and aggressive tactics – but if you were to remain relaxed and resourced, you could maintain responding appropriately to situations rather than overreacting.

From Reaction to Response

The difficulty for people with anger issues is that they are easily triggered and rise quickly to the bait. While this is

Your body becomes an extremely accessible barometer to manage the curve balls life throws.

keenly observed in exploders, imploders are just as much affected – they might not say as much, but internalizing their anger has an equally negative effect. Usually when we react to something, especially if our reaction is extreme, it indicates an unresolved trauma – a situation or trigger from the past that has never been dealt with. When we respond to a situation would be to say that we are being somewhat more measured. It's easier to respond rather than to react when you are feeling less stressed and more relaxed in your daily life.

React/Respond

I have created these two acronyms (explained on the following pages) to help you understand the difference between each impulse. The intention behind this is to give you an outline of the characteristics involved in the two different states of being. You may notice from the start that they both take up a very different position, which will equally lend a very different result. Perhaps you relate more to one than the other. If we're caught up in a 'react' mode it will take a fair amount of diligence and discipline to change our habit, but it's not impossible. First, let's identify the two approaches for clarity.

React

R = RESISTANCE

Resist the temptation to be 'right' or to 'win', to remain in control, or to be 'on top of your game'.

E = ENVY/EGO IDENTITY

Remind yourself that if your anger is excessive and disproportionate to the event, you are trying to take the superior role in an effort to keep yourself safe from pain.

A = ACCEPT

Accept that you are feeling anger and that it's ok to feel this way. Allow yourself to feel the feelings but not become overwhelmed by them.

C = CATASTROPHIZE

Remind your 'old' brain that you are safe and there is no need to go into high alert. There is no danger to your survival – you are just in a situation where you feel overwhelmed.

T = THINKING

If you recognize that your thoughts are negative and harmful, choose not to invest a lot of time into this way of thinking. Instead, engage in an activity that will shift you out of your negative state until such time as you have gained clarity.

Respond

R = REMAIN CALM

Connecting to your breath and purposefully slowing it down will help keep you in the here and now.

E = EMPATHIZE

Listen to the other person and see their point of view. Keep the bigger picture in mind. Keep your heart open. The other person is not the enemy, even though it feels that way.

S = SAFE

Keep reminding yourself that you are safe and no one is going to harm you. Keep breathing slowly.

P = PREPARED

Be sensitive to any changes in the situation and to the dynamic. If matters escalate, choose to walk away from the situation.

O = OBJECTIVITY

Stop, think, take a look at the big picture. Try to understand why the other person is behaving in that particular way. It's usually because their needs are not being met.

N = NOTICE

Notice what is going on for you as well as for the other person and try to create some emotional distance in order to reflect on and understand their behaviour.

D = DISCIPLINE

Remind yourself of the consequences and that the other person is not the enemy. Let go of being right and your attachment to winning.

Common Effects of Stress

These are some typical symptoms of stress. If you recognize any of them in yourself, make a note of them in your journal.

On Your Body

Headache	*Muscle tension or pain*
Chest pain	*Fatigue*
Change in sex drive	*Sleep problems*
Heart disease	*Indigestion problems*
Skin disorders	

On Your Mood

Anxiety	*Restlessness*
Lack of motivation	*Poor concentration*
Irritability or anger	*Sadness*
Depression	*Listlessness*

On Your Behaviour

Over- or under-eating	*Angry outbursts*
Drug or alcohol abuse	*Tobacco use*
Social withdrawal	

De-Stressing

Stress is often misperceived and misunderstood, with people failing to acknowledge the real impact it has on their lives. Stress in itself is not what causes the suffering – it's the anxious thoughts that drive the emotional distress in the body that are responsible.

People often think that anger is the driving force behind stress, but actually stress is anxiety-/fear-driven. Stress is created when we believe we have no control over situations. It might be true that we have very little control over the inevitable, but we do have control over our thoughts. We can train the brain to consider positive outcomes as opposed to fearing the worst. Rather than being at the constant mercy of stress, we can look at it from the perspective of what is getting in the way of us dealing with our stress.

Shaking the Apple Tree

Ask people to identify the major stressors that they face in their lives and it's not difficult for them to come up with a fairly conclusive list. However, what's more challenging – and more informative – is to get them to identify what gets in the way of reducing their stress levels. I've come up with a simple yet powerful method to do this, called 'Shaking the Apple Tree'.

I've used this term as a metaphor because it's the ripest apples that fall to the ground first, ready to eat. In the same way, you can use the easiest and most accessible information about yourself in order to make choices about what to do next and how best to manage that information. Using this process to explore what gets in the way of reducing stress becomes informative, then transformative, for two reasons:

1. You start to see how you create your own suffering.

2. If you can look at your resistance to making certain changes in your life and understand the insanity behind that, you can put simple and practical strategies in place to deal with your resistance.

For example, if you find being overweight stressful, the best thing to do is to eat healthier foods and exercise more. A simple solution – yes, of course! However, the problem lies not in the simplicity of the solution, but in the resistance to putting in place fundamental steps to manage the stress and anxiety we feel in relation to being overweight. The resistance is to letting go of the anxiety or even the suffering that not meeting this goal creates.

Identifying the Unconscious Drive

I am slightly overweight and could do with slimming down a bit. I know this – so what gets in the way of me taking exercise and moderating my eating? Looking into it more deeply, I could say that, in my case, I am addicted to the anxiety and the suffering of being overweight. In other words, if I got fit and lost weight, what would I replace the anxiety and suffering with? The obvious answer is — a sense of health, alertness and well-being! So do I get up in the morning and commit to exercising more and eating less? No. Why? Because on some level I prefer the pay-off of the anxiety, which reinforces some negative idea of myself and impacts on my self-esteem. That's why it's important to become aware of the unconscious drive — because in so doing I can consciously choose to move towards health and feel much better for it. Eventually there comes a point where it's not so much of a battle and exercising is a joy. Hence, tackling these two aspects — exposing our hidden motives and changing them as well as applying ourselves practically — is a potent combination. This is the reason why 'quick fixes' never work, because the hidden motive that drives the behaviour is never addressed.

The Underlying Factors

Working with course participants in recent years, I have discovered that there are five major underlying factors as to why we get so terribly stressed and then angry.

1. *Not making ourselves a priority in our own lives*
2. *Relinquishing control, or at times needing to take control*
3. *Not trusting ourselves or others*
4. *Seeking approval or trying to prove ourselves*
5. *Putting ourselves under too much pressure.*

Let's investigate these factors and see why they're so damaging to your self-esteem and how they amplify your stress.

1. *Not Making Yourself a Priority in Your Own Life*
People who lead stressful lives have no idea what it means to prioritize themselves. They prioritize everyone else and consider themselves last, if at all. In effect, this means that most of the time they're emotionally and psychologically under-resourced. Dealing with the experiences of their daily lives becomes overwhelming and, should this continue over a long period of time, it can take the smallest event to tip them over. When they do eventually find time to prioritize themselves, they're too exhausted and all they want to do is collapse into a sofa and numb out or sleep for ever. Looking deeper, the stress is often born out of the need to please everyone and they therefore over-extend themselves. In addition, they often feel stressed out by the levels of resentment they feel towards others because they seem to be doing everything all the time and nobody else is pulling their weight! By not making themselves a priority, they often lack in emotional nourishment, and are under-resourced and exhausted. Using the Shaking the Apple Tree method, we explore what's getting in the way of them not prioritizing themselves – and if they did prioritize themselves, how would their lives be different?

People who suffer from low self-esteem don't prioritize themselves. Their belief is that by caring and doing everything for others, they will get their positive strokes or a pat on the back and their self-esteem will be boosted – but this is a fallacy. No one else can boost or increase their self-esteem – only they can. Ironically, one of the best ways we can do this is to prioritize ourselves and make sure we attend to our own needs before anyone else's.

When I introduce this idea in my workshops, parents are the ones who look horrified and challenge my logic the most – understandably. I have to remind them that if they are emotionally and psychologically unfit, if they're running on empty, how can they really be there for their kids? All that happens is that parents end up feeling resentful because of the demands their children make on their time, energy, patience and love.

When you prioritize yourself and ensure you're resourced, being there for others is actually enjoyable and not a chore or a duty. You need to acknowledge that being responsible for your own vitality is of utmost importance. It's not about being selfish, it's about being mindful of what you can and cannot do, recognizing your limitations and learning to say no. In this way, what you are able to offer others comes from an authentic place within you. This holds as much value for *you* as the person giving as it does for the person receiving. It becomes a reciprocal exchange in day-to-day life and the pay-off is that you aren't exhausted by the engagement. In fact you're likely to feel happier and have more energy. Taking practical steps to make yourself a priority leaves you feeling better about yourself and instantly reduces your stress levels. The best thing is that if *you* are happier, people around you will feel happier. It's not a pleasant experience for family

members, friends or colleagues to be around someone who is often stressed. It feels toxic – because it is.

Now you can understand how important it is that you value your own vitality, be clear about what you can and cannot do, and see how that is of real benefit to everyone around you.

2. *Relinquishing Control*

This section is for all the control freaks reading this book. Trying to control everything is impossible – and you know it! Whether you want to admit it or not, you're already paying the price and dealing with the consequences. It leaves you exhausted, disorientated, overwhelmed, paranoid, resentful, stressed and – most importantly – living or working with you is a nightmare. You know this and the people around you know it even more, because they have to deal constantly with your neurosis. Relinquishing control is vital for your health, emotional well-being and self-esteem, and in so doing you will certainly reduce your stress and anxiety levels.

The reason you're a control freak is that you have never felt, and still don't feel, safe in the world. These are deep-

---

'Before you can learn to say "no", you have
to decide what to say "yes" to.'

ANON

---

seated feelings, the origins of which are found in the belly of childhood. If as a child your environment was unsafe, you had no choice but to develop certain skills and strategies to keep yourself safe and out of danger's way. This may have been a long-term experience or a particularly powerful one that could originate from within the family or school system. As a way of compensating for the overwhelming feeling of loss of power, control freaks have to take charge of their own safety. The problem is that the need for control extends to that of other people in a neurotic way. This has a way of permeating every single aspect of life and can be experienced by many as stifling. In childhood this behaviour may not have manifested, but in adulthood – where we have more influence over people – this type of behaviour really impacts negatively on people.

We contaminate people with our obsessive controlling behaviour. In some circumstances it may be seen as helpful, but not when you obsessively take charge of every single minute detail in your own life and everyone else's!

The reality is that trying to control every little thing is virtually impossible and when things don't go the way you want them to, it leads to stress. Stress fuels anger and someone will eventually feel the full brunt of your distress.

Asking a control freak to relinquish control is like asking a driver to take his hands off the steering wheel when the car is out of control. Letting go of that wheel takes a tremendous amount of trust – firstly in yourself and then in others. It's taking that leap of faith into the unknown – throwing yourself off a cliff trusting you will fly, knowing that gravity is your obstacle. You can put everything in place that you need to, but you still have to trust that you will fly, that you will defy gravity.

The constant effort of trying to control everything – every little detail – is one of the most significant stressors in people. It's an enormous internal pressure driven by the fear of feeling powerless. But if you don't let go, you may never fly and you would miss out on a whole realm of experience. Some of you might say that you're happy with this, but it's not fair or helpful when it infiltrates the lives of others. This is where your behaviour starts to be toxic and suffocating.

I've noticed that people who have anger issues tend to need to be in control, no matter what the consequence. You may need to find a way to learn to trust that letting go does not mean you'll die a terrible death. Relinquishing control might mean you can enjoy spontaneity, creativity and excitement, increase your vitality and be open to feeling more relaxed. This is deeply nourishing for the soul and you will experience an increased sense of joy in your life.

3. *Not Trusting Yourself or Others*
If you find it hard to trust yourself you will be risk-averse, and you won't trust others if you find it difficult to let them into your emotional realm. A lot of angry people have trust issues. When we don't trust, we limit our lives.

EXPLORING TRUST

Let's investigate the relationship you have to trust. Be brutally honest. Write your findings down in your journal.

1. What don't you trust about yourself?

2. What gets in the way of trusting others?

3. How do you think you came to these internal conclusions? Where do you imagine you got these messages from, and who might have given them to you?

People learn not to trust because of the messages they once received, such as 'you are not capable of being trusted' or 'others are not to be trusted'. It's very difficult to have reciprocal relationships if we don't trust each other. Once you get caught in your own mistrust, you can begin to feel alone, isolated and possibly depressed (remember, depression is anger turned inwards). It's quite possible to spend long periods of time in this way of being, without realizing that you have limited trust in yourself and other people.

At a very deep level, people who have been angry for years feel let down – they have felt so betrayed by events in the past that to trust life is almost impossible. They use their anger as a way to control their environment and as a defence to avoid being hurt again. Unfortunately, being angry and scary means

TAKING RISKS TO BUILD TRUST

A good strategy to build your trust levels is to start taking very small risks. Make a list of risks that you *could* take but are too afraid to. Start with the little risks and name five. Include this list in your journal and work towards achieving them. Write down how that made you feel. Once you have completed that task, make a list of slightly bigger risks. Set about achieving them and try to be realistic around timelines. Continue with this strategy. As you survive these risks, you will find that your courage increases. As your courage increases, your trust in yourself and others will increase too, and your self-esteem will get a positive boost.

it's very difficult for other people to trust *you*, and being unable to communicate your needs leaves you feeling unheard.

Eventually, lacking in trust altogether, life becomes an empty void – allowing people in emotionally is difficult, and allowing yourself to be vulnerable is just not an option. This creates a barren internal wasteland. If you've been angry for so long that people learn to keep you at a distance and shut you out, and if you have had to bear the brunt of another's anger, you become terrified to show how desperate and fragile you are for fear of further attack, rejection and abandonment.

Learning to trust that everything will be ok, that you can do better, that it's not all your fault and that there is more to life are some of the greatest challenges. It may feel all too difficult and overwhelming, but this again is where getting support or developing a mindful practice helps you. Being present and available in this moment only is what matters. There is a lot of power in that.

If you experienced a lot of trauma in early childhood, the likelihood is that your brain will be hard-wired differently. You will be highly attuned to any perceived threat and therefore live in a constant state of high alert or hyper-vigilance. In reality, what this means is that from a very young age your central nervous system was set at this particular barometer. Add an increase in your stress levels and you'll be dealing with more stimuli than most. You may already have an increase in the stress hormone cortisol flowing through your system, so increasing it further with added stress will significantly reduce your ability to feel safe. A sense of real safety and therefore relaxation is near impossible if you have never experienced them before on a visceral level. You would just come to understand that life is highly strained, charged, alert, manic. Accessing very deep places of stillness or ease – a place of safety and comfort – is utterly absent from your psyche. In fact, you may never have even posed the question. Hyper-vigilance is your standard and people come to know you for your idiosyncratic ways.

The tragedy is that in not being given a safe world to grow up in, you continue to feel threatened into your adulthood and this becomes your demise. You either threaten others or control them. Unfortunately, this only keeps you distant from the deep safety and connection you crave – however, it is possible to establish a different outlook, heal wounds and work towards a future that encompasses respect, love and interdependence.

If you identify with any of the high arousal indicators (see box below), it would be beneficial to become more attuned to your body. Start to understand the difference between arousal and relaxation. Develop the dialogue. Mindfulness meditation and mindfulness body scans (see Chapter Three) will help, and – in more extreme situations – tension and trauma

---

High Arousal Indicators

Indicators of high arousal include:

- *Being easily startled when there is no threat whatsoever*
- *Constantly looking over your shoulder or feeling the need to be on high alert*
- *Finding the slightest noise is overwhelming and irritating*
- *Always expecting the worst possible outcomes*
- *Being overly controlling towards your environment*
- *Trying to relax, but never quite being able to*
- *Insomnia.*

release bodywork or trauma incident reduction (TIR). In effect you will be encouraging your central nervous system to rest and digest your experiences rather than be constantly tuned into a hyper-aroused one. This *is* possible, and will release you from years of stress – you will be amazed by how much more vitality you will feel in your system. This will also in effect set you free from the internal constraints you feel and give you back your life. It will raise your confidence and you will develop the resources to cope with life's curve balls.

Mindfulness can allow us to be with the things we fear without being overwhelmed by them. By giving our fears and anxieties our attention, we can shift our relationship with them, rather than compulsively running away.

The psychotherapist Fritz Perls described it perfectly: 'Anxiety is the gap between the now and the later.' Eckhart Tolle asks us: 'Where is your attention? Do you live in "the later" more than the now? Then you are trapped in your thoughts, because what is the future other than a thought in your head? Only your thoughts can make you anxious! Bring your attention to the now. Seeing, listening, breathing, feeling the aliveness inside your body.'

It is beneficial to keep reminding yourself of the positive qualities that learning to trust yourself will bring:

- It will immediately increase your self-esteem.
- It will give you freedom to experience new things.
- It will allow other people to get closer to you.

- It will reduce your stress levels enormously and enable you to feel more relaxed and nourished.
- As you start to trust yourself, you can begin to learn to trust others.
- You will take more risks and enjoy the freedom it brings.
- You won't have to feel so alone and misunderstood.

See if you can come up with a few more and make a note of them in your journal.

4. *Seeking Approval or Trying to Prove Yourself*
If we have low self-esteem, one of the ways we try to gain esteem is by seeking the approval of others. We spend a lot of wasted time and energy trying to acquire positive strokes to prove to ourselves that we are worthy of praise, that we're good people. People who are invested in getting approval from others will always reach the point where they don't get the positive strokes they were looking for, and this can then be a trigger for anger.

Constantly seeking approval or having to prove ourselves has an impact on how hard we drive ourselves. If you identify with this, you know how exhausted you can land up feeling. It means you are over-sensitized to doing things to the best of your (sometimes limited) ability, to going over and beyond the call of duty (perfectionism being an understatement), and to never really being satisfied with what you've produced. The stress is relentless and you end up becoming fatigued. It can

> **EXPLORING THE NEED TO PROVE YOURSELF**
>
> Take some time to reflect on the following:
> - *Why do you feel the need to prove yourself to others or yourself?*
> - *What would happen if you were to stop seeking approval from others or trying so hard to prove yourself?*
> - *What would be the worst-case scenario if you changed this behaviour?*
>
> Set aside some time to contemplate these questions and write down your insights in your journal.

feel like hitting a wall at very fast speed and then suddenly stopping, paralysed with exhaustion. If you did not receive the recognition you were looking for as a young child, you may have interpreted this as 'I am unlovable' or 'I'm not worthy of being loved'. This will directly impact on your self-esteem and it's possible that you will over-compensate if you bought into those messages.

If you believe you need the approval of others in order to feel good about yourself, not receiving that approval can trigger deep-seated anxieties and increase your levels of stress. In the long term, this can lead to depression or acting out in anger, depending on your personality type – and whether you're an imploder or exploder. Either way, suppressing the need for recognition or looking for it externally will eventually find a way of sabotaging your life. You could consider what would happen if you were to stop seeking approval or trying so hard to prove yourself (see box on page 77).

Initially you might discover that you upset a few people because they're used to your full attention and now they are not getting it. The benefit to you, though, is that you will lower your stress levels significantly and probably feel less exhausted.

I have worked with many people who are obsessed with seeking approval, and the sad thing is they're not even aware of it. Once they attend our programme and run through the 'Shaking the Apple Tree' process, they realize how much the need for approval drives them and also how it starts to fuel their stress – which eventually turns to anger. There is something very empowering about letting go of this need.

These are some of the benefits you are likely to feel:
- There will be less of an emotional investment in others liking you.
- You will find yourself *not* having to make excuses – or defend yourself, for that matter.
- You will have a lot more energy just to get on with the things you really enjoy doing.
- A whole new world of choices will open up for you because you will start to choose to do things for yourself instead of for other people in order to get your positive strokes.

Regardless of whether you are an imploder or exploder, putting yourself under pressure is one of the root causes of anger.

- People will find you more relaxed, far less needy, and a pleasure to be around because you won't be stressed and miserable. A big bonus to all concerned!
- You will begin to enjoy your own company and discover that you quite like who you've become now that you've dropped the drama that goes with proving yourself to the world.
- Your self-esteem will increase by doing things for yourself rather than needing the approval of others.

5. *Putting Yourself Under Too Much Pressure*
Regardless of whether you are an imploder or exploder, putting yourself under pressure is one of the root causes of anger. The question here is – why do we do this? What is it about our psyches that drives us so hard? I have never met an angry person who has denied the fact that they put themselves under a lot of pressure. People who seek the approval of others and who spend all their time and energy trying to prove themselves are under pressure. The problem with this is that it eventually becomes a habit. We're driven to achieve perfection.

Look at it from this point of view – if I can do everything perfectly, then I am not open to being told off, shouted at, shamed or blamed. If I can achieve perfection, I have proved to everyone (including myself) that I am of value, of worth and acceptable. If I do everything perfectly I can get the acclaim I deserve. Unfortunately, the price we pay for putting ourselves under pressure for long periods of time is stress – to ourselves, and consequently to others who live or work in our orbit. This way of thinking can go so unchecked that sometimes we even fail to recognize that we hold the same expectation of others. It's only when people fail to meet our expectations that all hell breaks loose.

Caught in the constant effort of seeking approval or trying to prove ourselves, we lose sight of the real cost to our lives. In effect, if we were not so invested in proving our merits to the world, we would be more selective about what we really want to do rather than feel we 'should' do. We would have more time for ourselves, to spend relaxing and enjoying life's precious little moments hanging out with family and friends.

Not making yourself a priority, not taking control or perhaps needing to relinquish control, not trusting yourself or others, seeking approval or trying to prove yourself all contribute to the overwhelming sense of being under too much pressure. For many, just to consider what would happen if they did not keep up the pressure raises their stress levels even more!

OPENING TO STILLNESS & SOLITUDE

Stress & Self-Esteem

Stress is linked to low self-esteem. If you have healthy self-esteem you do not allow yourself to get stressed to the point that it manifests as anger or physical illness. You are able to recognize when something is healthy for you and when it is not and then move towards making conscious choices about what you allow to affect you.

I am often asked, 'What is the difference between self-esteem and confidence?' A good example lies in the way I describe myself. I might be an excellent facilitator and presenter and feel very confident in my skills, abilities and talents – but that does not necessarily mean I have a strong, healthy sense of self-esteem. Healthy self-esteem is defined by the value I place on myself, by how worthy I feel I am of love, appreciation, acceptance, respect, etc... Self-esteem lies at the very core of our being and determines what we are willing to accept, or not accept. It defines how we operate in the world; what we stand for and the boundaries we set around us. A healthy self-esteem sets the ground from which we operate. Instead of constantly seeking assurance from outside ourselves, we feel innately assured and are therefore able to offer the world this quality too. It increases our capacity to manage life's stresses and strains because we don't interpret life's knocks to mean something about us.

> 'You yourself, as much as anybody in the entire universe, deserve your love and affection.'
>
> BUDDHA

An Exercise in De-Stressing

I invite you to investigate these five key underlying factors and determine your relationship to each. Start by looking at your resistance to:

1. *Not making ourselves a priority in our own lives*
2. *Relinquishing control, or at times needing to take control*
3. *Not trusting ourselves or others*
4. *Seeking approval or trying to prove ourselves*
5. *Putting ourselves under too much pressure.*

Once you have identified which underlying factor/stressor above is most pertinent to you, investigate it further by using the Shaking the Apple Tree process below. (It may be that you want to run this process through with all five stressors).

There are two parts to this exercise. Firstly, identify the biggest stressor in your life and note it in your journal. Then, in relation to that stressor, ask yourself the following questions:

1. *What do I need to let go of?*
2. *What do I need to admit?*
3. *What do I need to acknowledge?*
4. *What do I need to accept?*
5. *What do I need to give up?*

EXAMPLE 1

My biggest stressor is putting myself under so much pressure! In order to stop putting myself under so much pressure, I need to:

- *Let go* of thinking I am superhuman.
- *Admit* that I tend to believe I have to do everything myself and not ask for help.
- *Acknowledge* that my world won't collapse if I give myself a break.
- *Accept* that taking the pressure off myself gives me a lot more time to relax and enjoy myself with family and friends.
- *Give up* believing that everything needs to be done right now and accept that some things can wait.

Now look at the list above and decide which statement really stands out as the most significant for you. Circle or highlight it and move on to the second part of this process, a series of questions and answers arising from that statement.

EXAMPLE 2

The statement that really stands out for me is:

'Believing that everything needs to be done right now.'

Q *If I stopped believing that everything has to be done right now, how would my life be different?*

A I would stop putting pressure on myself.

Q *If I stopped putting pressure on myself, how would my life be different?*

A I would probably feel calmer and more relaxed.

Q *If I felt calmer and more relaxed, how would my life be different?*

A I would be pleasant to be around and the people in my life would be happier.

Q *And if I were more pleasant to be around and the people in my life were happier, how would my life be different?*

A I would be happy!

Bingo! That's the answer we all want.

Through this process, you may start to notice several things about yourself:

1. *Your emotional investment in how the world sees you*
2. *How you create your own suffering without considering the implications for yourself or others*
3. *How stress impacts on your self-esteem.*

OPENING TO STILLNESS & SOLITUDE

> 'Believe nothing because a wise man said it.
> Believe nothing because it is generally held.
> Believe nothing because it is written.
> Believe nothing because it is said to be divine.
> Believe nothing because someone else believes it.
> But believe only what you yourself know to be true.'
>
> BUDDHA

By learning to manage your neurotic impulses through applying what you learn here on a daily basis and letting the noise settle, you will eventually become increasingly open to stillness and silence. I find it amazing that my whole being now yearns for this, and without it I would find it impossible to remain relaxed and happy. Stillness and silence have become nourishing friends, and solitude a welcome retreat.

In each part of the exercise, be honest with yourself and give yourself time to reflect and introspect. Make notes in your journal and enjoy the journey. If you apply yourself based on the above, you will be surprised by how quickly you can align yourself to a new way of being in the world. Experiment with what you have learnt, keep your mind and heart open to the process and, if it works for you, then model silence and solitude and healthy anger so that others may want to do the same.

CHAPTER THREE

MEDITATION AS MEDICINE FOR THE SOUL

The most reliable and immediately accessible way for you to recognize how you are feeling – and therefore in turn make a judgement call on how well equipped you are to manage the day – is to tune in to your body. Being mindful of your energy levels, stresses and strains and general well-being gives you an indication of what you are, or perhaps will not be, capable of facing. All it takes is some time to train your brain and get into the practice of using your body sensations to guide you. Meditation is the ideal tool.

Control Your Internal Environment

◆

Becoming aware of the different states your body can be in – relaxed, peaceful, hyped-up – is a resource you can rely on. Likewise, it's just as important to become familiar with what it means to be calm and peaceful, for as you move out of this place you lose your equanimity.

SITUATIONS WILL BE EVER MORE MISMANAGED if you cannot approach them from a place of being resourced and maintaining a certain neutrality. In an ideal world we would all love to be able to maintain that sense of calm and objectivity – but we are not in control of our external environment. We can, however, have a certain measure of control over our internal environment. So, when we find ourselves about to fly off the handle we have to bring our awareness to the situation and recognize that we have choices. I'm the first to acknowledge how difficult it is to step back and slow things down when your heart and body are surging with stress hormones and adrenaline. That's why I'd like to introduce you to the following meditations as tools to reduce your reactivity.

◆

All meditations in this book can be found, some in audio form, on *www.angermindfulness.co.uk*.

◆

> **Body & Mind**
>
> The meditations in this chapter are designed to let you first explore the sensations in your body before moving on to examine your feelings. Only when you explore, examine and begin to understand the workings of the reactive body and whirring mind can you move towards balance.
>
> Carry out these exercises on a regular basis, for at least 60 days – a daily practice is ideal, and if possible choose a regular time such as first thing in the morning or before bed. Practise for the length of time suggested in each exercise – it's usually best to start with a shorter time and work up, although you may find yourself able to do some of the exercises more quickly with practice.

Volume Control

I like to compare the intense surge of sensations you can feel when angry to a volume control button. In this way you can use the image to focus on turning down the volume.

This exercise is all about learning to regulate the intensity of your feelings, especially your anger. Allow about 10 to 20 minutes for the exercise, depending on the intensity of your anger. The more attention you give to the process, the better you will begin to feel.

Close your eyes and visualize a built-in volume control button. Recall an angry incident that is still fresh in your mind and connect to the feelings you felt then. Locate where the sensations are in your body, where it feels the most intense, and in its place imagine the volume control button.

Examples of what can happen in the body when anger is triggered include:

- *Discomfort, especially in your stomach*
- *Tension in your shoulders, jaw, neck, arms and fists*
- *Headache or even migraine*
- *Sweaty palms*
- *Feeling generally unrelaxed*
- *A metallic taste in your mouth*
- *Tiredness and irritability*
- *Nervousness and jumpiness.*

Identify the sensation that feels most familiar to you. Now pinpoint where you feel your volume marker is, with a maximum setting of 10 and a minimum of 0. From this point, visualize yourself slowly turning down the volume. Notice what happens to your body as you do this. How do your body

---

'The body needs material food every day.

The soul needs spiritual food.'

ANON

---

sensations change? If you feel you have experienced no change, turn the button even more slowly or repeat the exercise until you feel more relaxed.

Make a note of your experience in your journal.

Body Scan Meditation

After completing the volume control exercise, try the body scan and progressive relaxation muscle process below. This is a simple and effective body scan meditation to train your focus while remaining mindful and open to any sensation that arises. If you encounter pain or muscle tension, try to accept rather than minimize or control it.

Practise this meditation for as long as you like – 20 minutes is a good starting point.

Here are a few key pointers to make it more effective:

- DON'T EAT ANYTHING TOO HEAVY – An hour before doing this meditation, avoid heavy food and stimulants such as tea, coffee, sweets, alcohol, etc., as these can get in the way of supporting a relaxed body and mind.
- DIM THE LIGHTS OR CLOSE THE CURTAINS – If that's not possible, you might consider blindfolding yourself.
- SWITCH OFF YOUR MOBILE PHONE – If you have an alarm you might like to set it for ten-minute intervals, so that you're aware of time as you go through the meditation, but do keep the volume low and choose an ascending alarm if possible – you don't want to startle your relaxed state.

- **WEAR COMFORTABLE CLOTHING** – Choose loose-fitting clothes and take off your shoes.
- **BE COMFORTABLE** – If lying on your back, try placing a pillow under your knees to avoid strain on your lower back – some people find this more restful. If you're uncomfortable with your legs out straight, you might like to bend your knees and place your feet flat on the floor. If lying down isn't comfortable, try sitting in a firm chair.
- **TUNE IN TO BEING MINDFUL** – Detach yourself from any distractions, then gently, patiently focus your awareness on your breathing and body.
- **DON'T BE ANXIOUS** – Don't worry about doing this right. Let go of any expectations. The fact that you are doing it is what matters.

Practising Body Scanning
When you are comfortable, take your attention to your breathing and breathe slowly and deeply through your nose. Feel your abdomen rise as your diaphragm expands to take air into your lungs. Make sure your chest only rises a little.

Continue breathing slowly as you bring your attention to your left foot. Curl and release your toes once. Focus your awareness on your toes and foot.

As you breathe in, slowly begin to scan your left leg from your foot to your knee, and up to your thigh.

Now just follow your breath out, down your thigh to your

knee, and down to your foot and to the tips of your toes. Do this three times, then take your attention from your breath and remain focused on your foot.

Experience the sensations in your foot for a few seconds. Scan your left lower leg. Be aware of any tension or discomfort you can feel and accept it. Now begin to slowly scan through your thigh. If any thoughts arise during this time, that's okay. Gently return your attention to your breath.

Now shift your awareness to your right foot and toes. Curl and release your toes once. Focus your awareness on your toes and foot.

As you breathe in, slowly begin to scan your right leg from your foot to your knee, and up to your thigh... Breathe out slowly and scan back down slowly. Do this three times.

Take your time, don't rush this experience. Now take your attention from the breath and just be with your foot and toes.

Become aware of any sensation in your foot and toes, your calf, your thigh. Allow yourself to be with all sensations and notice what happens. Relax.

Now turn your attention to your stomach. Feel it rising as you take a breath in and sinking as you breathe out. Notice your breath gently flowing through your nostrils. You might even notice your heart rate slowing down as you relax more. Remain focused on your stomach and breathe gently in and out. Tune in to any sensations you might be experiencing and just go deeper and deeper into relaxing.

Now move your attention to your left hand, fingers and arm. Follow the same procedure as you did with your left leg. First make a fist and focus your attention on your left hand. Keep breathing slowly and gently.

Scan through the length of your left arm, up through your chest and down your right arm to your right hand and fingers. Move your fingers lightly. Notice any sensations. Be aware of your breathing. Relax. Do this three times.

Now bring your attention to your chest. Scan up through your neck and face. Very gently wriggle your jaw, clench your teeth and release the tension. Experience the sensation in your jaw and your throat. Keep breathing gently and scan the back of your head. Become aware of how your head is supported by the floor or, if you're sitting in a chair, how it's supported by your neck and shoulders.

Draw your attention to the top of your scalp, relax and notice your breathing. Do this three times.

Now disconnect from your body and all its parts. Take a deep breath in. Notice how everything remains connected, as you lie or sit there totally relaxed. Become aware of how you are feeling and notice any new sensations. Just allow it to be. These sensations are different aspects of who you are. They come and go, fluctuating according to your moods and what's happening around you.

Take another deep breath in and a slow deep breath out. Lie or sit still for a few more minutes and experience your body in this state of relaxation. Now bring your attention to your surroundings. Look around you. Sit or stand and look around you.

Make notes in your journal to help you remember your experience of this meditation.

Progressive Muscle Relaxation Technique

The progressive muscle relaxation process is popular in anger management and stress management programmes. It's a systematic technique for achieving a deep state of relaxation, developed by Dr Edmund Jacobson over fifty years ago. Dr Jacobson found that a muscle could be relaxed by first tensing it for a few seconds and then releasing it. Tensing and releasing various muscle groups throughout the body produces a deep state of relaxation. This might seem hard to believe, but just follow these simple guidelines – you will be amazed.

- Practise at least 20 to 30 minutes per day.
- Find a quiet place to practise, making sure you won't be distracted. Switch off your phone so you won't be disturbed.
- Practise at a regular time of day whenever possible. This might be first thing in the morning or last thing at night.
- Practise between meals. Being hungry or digesting food can sometimes disrupt deep relaxation.
- Lie down on the floor, sofa or bed in a comfortable position. Your head and body need to be supported. If you feel tired it will be better to sit in a comfortable chair or recliner. If you

lie down, place a pillow beneath your knees for further support. The idea is to be as comfortable as you possibly can to experience the full effect of the relaxation consciously, but without nodding off!

- Wear comfortable, loose-fitting clothes and remove your shoes, watch, glasses or contact lenses and jewellery.
- Let go of worries and concerns. Decide to be fully present in the moment and do not allow anything to come in the way of this experience.
- The most important element is to take on a passive, detached approach. Adopt the attitude 'just let it unfold' and don't worry about how well you are doing the technique. The success of this exercise depends entirely on you letting go of everything. Don't even try to relax, do it well or control your body. Just go with the process and see what happens.

The Technique

Progressive muscle relaxation involves tensing and relaxing each of the 16 different muscle groups in the body. You need to tense hard enough to feel the tension, but not hard enough to strain yourself. Do this for about ten seconds. And then instantly relax the muscle for 15–20 seconds.

Notice the difference between a tense muscle and a relaxed muscle. Then move on to the next muscle group. You may find it helpful to say to yourself, 'Relax', 'Let go', 'Release the tension, let it flow away', or a phrase of your own between each phase of the relaxation process. You might repeat the same phrase each time, like a mantra, or switch between phases. During each part of the exercise, stay focused on your muscles. When your awareness drifts, come back to the muscle group you're working on.

The sequence initially takes about 20–30 minutes, but with practice you may decrease this to 15–20 minutes.

Points to remember:

- Lie or sit in a quiet and comfortable space.
- When you tense the different muscle groups, make sure you do so with vigour but without straining, or you could end up hurting yourself. Do this for seven to ten seconds. As you tense, count 'one-thousand-one', 'one-thousand-two' and so on, to count off the seconds.
- Stay concentrated and focused on what you are experiencing, and as you do so notice how each particular muscle group builds up with tension. In your mind's eye, visualize the muscle group being tensed up.
- On releasing the muscles, relax instantly and enjoy the immediate gratification of the release of tension. Relax for 15–20 seconds, then move on to the next group of muscles.
- Allow other muscle groups in your body to be relaxed while you are working on a specific muscle group.
- Tense and relax each muscle group once. If a particular area feels very tight or stiff, tense and relax the muscles two or three more times, waiting 15–20 seconds between each cycle.

CLEARING THE RED MIST

❋

1. Take three deep breaths through your nostrils, slowly exhaling through your mouth. Imagine any tension you are holding in your body draining away as you exhale.

2. Clench both fists. Hold tightly, without straining, for seven to ten seconds then let go for 15–20 seconds. Repeat for all muscle groups.

3. Tense your biceps by pulling your forearms up towards your shoulders and 'making a muscle' with both arms. Hold for seven to ten seconds, then relax for 15–20 seconds.

4. Tense your triceps, on the undersides of your upper arms, by stretching your arms out straight in front of you and locking your elbows tight. Hold then relax and notice what you experience. Keep breathing.

5. Raise your eyebrows up high to tighten the muscles in your forehead. Slightly tense the muscles in the back of your neck at the same time. Hold, then relax. Notice how the tension in your forehead muscles drains away as you relax that muscle group.

6. Tighten the muscles around your eyes by closing your eyelids tightly. Hold, then relax. Notice a softening of tension. Keep breathing.

7. Open your mouth as wide as you can to create tension in your jaw. Hold and relax. Let your lips part slightly and your jaw hang loose.

8. Focus your attention on the muscles in the back of your neck – gently tighten them by pulling your head as far back as possible, as if trying to touch your back. Tense the muscles in your neck. Hold…and relax. For many, the neck holds the most tension, so I suggest you tense and relax this area twice.

9. Take two deep breaths and just allow the weight of your head to drop straight down into your shoulders, or feel the weight of your head on the floor if you are lying down.

10. Tense your shoulders by lifting them up towards your ears. Hold the tension here, then drop and relax.

11. Push your shoulder blades back towards each other and experience the tightness. Hold, then relax. As with the neck, the shoulder blades can hold a lot of tension, so you might wish to repeat this process twice.

12. Take a deep breath to tighten the muscles around your chest. Hold, then slowly release. Notice the tension in your chest drain away as you exhale.

13. Breathe in and then pull in your stomach muscles tightly. Hold, then relax.

14. Arch your lower back and tighten the muscles. Hold, then relax. (Leave this out if you have lower back problems.)

15. Clench your buttocks together and then tense the muscles. Hold, then relax.

16. Tighten your thigh muscles. Hold, then relax completely. Do this twice as well.

17. Pull your toes towards you as far as you can to tighten your calf muscles without getting cramp. Hold, then relax.

18. Curl your toes in and hold the tension in your feet. Hold, then relax.

19. Scan your whole body and notice any more tension in any of the muscle groups. Wherever you feel tension, practise tightening and relaxing those muscles twice more.

Take some time to write down your experience in your journal.

Remain Vigilant

In my workshops, I often hear people say things like: 'If I had just a couple of seconds more to manage my anger, even that would've made a huge difference to how I behaved' or 'If I could just catch myself a few seconds before the moment happens, I could at least prepare myself for the impact and contain my outburst' or 'Sometimes my reactions are so fast I cannot even stop what's coming out of my mouth, I just black out and say things I regret later'.

I'm sure those are statements that many can relate to. The strategy for controlling your anger is to remain vigilant at all times to monitoring your stress levels. Educate yourself by tuning in to your body sensations and practise de-stressing by using the visualizations already given – as we saw in the previous chapter, managing your stress will help you to manage your anger. Monitor the difference in your body and mind – you may begin to notice that holding an awareness of your body sensations becomes increasingly accessible in any given moment. If you notice tension in your body, observe where it is and what might be the cause of it. You might, for example, notice that from one moment to the next there has been a sudden increase in tension in your chest. In this moment you could ask if the tension is related to anxiety (fear-based) or whether there has been a trigger for anger. Having early access to what is going on in your body is a useful resource for managing the intensity of your feelings.

TUNING IN TO YOURSELF

Preparing others by letting them know how you really felt before you became overwhelmed by intense feelings would go a long way towards managing challenging situations.

Here is an example of a short and easy exercise that will help you to develop the discipline of establishing a daily mindfulness practice.

Q *What am I doing right now?*
A Distracting myself from the task at hand.

Q *How do I feel right now?*
A Scared and angry.

Q *What is happening in my body right now?*
A I feel a tension in my head and neck and have butterflies in my stomach.

Q *What attention do I need to give myself right now?*
A A 20-minute mindfulness meditation, write in my journal, and if necessary call a friend for emotional support.

If you are aware of what you are feeling, thinking and experiencing in your body, moment to moment, this is the most powerful resource you have in controlling your anger.

How Are You?

It is all too easy to lose focus on what is happening in our internal world, on how we are feeling physically and emotionally. Next time someone asks 'How are you?', take the opportunity to tune in to yourself, take a moment to reflect — and then give an honest answer.

DEPENDING ON WHO IT IS and the nature of the relationship, when someone asks how I am, I will divulge exactly what I'm feeling and thinking and sometimes even include how my body feels in that moment. Most people tend to say things like 'I'm fine, okay, alright, good, not bad, tired, hungry', which is simply part of our social discourse. However, why not look at these moments as an opportunity to be mindful of where we're truly at in ourselves? If we can give ourselves permission to share that information and by so doing invite the other person to equally take stock, then we'd all be the better for it.

If it's really not appropriate or you don't feel comfortable, at least you can mentally take cognizance. Either way, I use the opportunity to do an internal body scan and check in with myself, and often it's then simply letting the other person know that I'm happy, sad, hurt or even scared. For me, those three most commonly used words in our daily conversations hold the key to becoming ever more present to ourselves and those we encounter.

Feeling Compass

To help expand your emotional repertoire beyond 'not bad, good, fine, alright, okay, tired, hungry, splendid', etc., I'd like to introduce you to the 'feeling compass', which I teach to my workshop and course participants. Without any doubt, 90 per cent of participants seem to be disassociated or disconnected from most of their feelings apart from anger. It's not that they don't feel anything – they do, but they are not able to communicate and express what they feel in healthy and meaningful ways. If they're exploders, they're dumping all over everyone and if they're imploders, they're repressing their feelings so much that it can often lead to depression.

At the British Association of Anger Management, we use eight 'feeling' words, which are: angry, sad, hurt, scared, peaceful, powerful, happy, shame. This is rather controversial, because according to many American theorists and academics we are born with only four feelings:

1. MAD (*angry*) 2. SAD (*sad*) 3. GLAD (*happy*) 4. BAD (*scared*)

The rest are all considered emotions. Some international theorists suggest there is no difference between a feeling and an emotion – feelings are synonymous with emotions and cannot be separated. This is a hotly debated subject and hundreds of thousands of words have been written on it. Please bear in mind that I am keeping the information here to a bare minimum in order for readers to get a broad sense of it.

Other theorists suggest that a feeling is different from an emotion and the difference is that an emotion (e-motion) is energy in motion. For example, a person might cry, but that does not mean they are sad or hurt – they might be happy because they have just won a million pounds on the lottery. A person who is screaming and shouting might be no longer expressing their anger, but showing outright aggression towards another person. My understanding is that a feeling is an internal experience, a 'felt' sense of something, and an emotion is an outward expression of the feeling.

I decided to keep it very simple, easy to understand and apply. The eight feelings that BAAM works with are partially represented by a mix of feeling and emotional words (we consider everything else as emotions). These are detailed overleaf.

After each explanation, I've provided examples of 'emotions' words that might otherwise be used to describe feelings. These are intended to guide you towards identifying your true feelings and emotions when engaging in the practice.

You can close your eyes to the things you do not want to see, but you cannot close your heart to the things you do not want to feel.

Finding What Works for You

In 2005 we ran our first series of stress management and mindfulness workshops for previous participants and diploma students on our Beating Anger programmes.

The workshops included a whole series of meditations, some of which are included in this book. One attendee felt that, for him, it was the missing link in managing his anger and stress. In a subsequent one-to-one session, he expressed his belief that the 'Loving Kindness' meditation (see pages 116–117) was what had helped him to deal with the guilt and shame that had burdened him for years.

Another client said the Body Scan meditation (see pages 91–95) helped her to focus her attention away from her anger. She felt that although the previous work she had done had gone a long way to helping her manage her temper, she was still preoccupied with malicious thoughts towards her father, but the body scan was an ideal distraction and helped her to develop a more relaxed relationship with her body.

Those who practise mindful meditation will find they feel kinship with some exercises and not others. You need to discover what works for you. I have personally found that constantly tuning in to my feelings is very helpful. I allow what I am feeling to just be and remind myself that distressing feelings will pass, like the clouds in the sky.

1. ANGRY

People use many words to describe anger and, if we look at it in terms of a spectrum, low-threshold anger might be irritation and high-threshold anger is physical violence. We tend to express anger by saying things like 'I feel pissed off with him' or 'I'm very annoyed that he did that' or 'I lost my temper with her' or 'I just saw red and lost it'.

The challenge is to be clear and direct and to say 'I'm angry with you'. That is the healthiest and cleanest way to express anger. Telling someone you are upset or disappointed means absolutely nothing. These two words are just a smokescreen for our true feelings. They don't actually say anything about how we feel – in fact, they give a mixed message, which is confusing, and makes it even harder for the other person to understand exactly what it is that you feel – especially children. For example, if you say to a child that you feel 'upset and disappointed', they will immediately feel ashamed of themselves. It's critical to be able to express feelings clearly, especially anger. This avoids mixed messages and game playing and helps to resolve situations more effectively.

If we can move away from language that is shaming or blaming, we stand a better chance of being heard. If a person becomes immediately reactionary or defensive, it's very difficult to get them to listen and cooperate with you. Let's look at how our communications can become habitual and how they hardly ever start with how we truly feel.

You never listen to me

Rather than saying, 'I feel sad when you don't listen to me and I'm aware there are many times I don't listen to you.'

You always interrupt me when I'm speaking to you

Rather than saying, 'I feel hurt and angry when you interrupt me. Please stop doing that as it breaks my concentration.'

You should stop just thinking about yourself and think about me for a change

Rather than saying, 'I feel sad when you don't take my feelings into consideration.'

- LOW-THRESHOLD ANGER – *irritated, agitated, frustrated*
- HIGH-THRESHOLD ANGER – *shouting, bullying, physical displays of anger / violence*

2. SAD

Sadness becomes apparent when there is loss or a sense of loss involved, and people are more likely to use the smokescreen words 'upset' or 'disappointed' than the word 'sad'. 'Upset' or 'disappointed' could equally mean sad or angry. It might be that you don't like to be open and honest about your feelings because you believe it's a weakness and it leaves you feeling vulnerable. However, in reality our strength lies in our vulnerability and in accepting the challenge to take care of our needs. It does take courage to reveal our true feelings in a way that is clear for the other person to understand, yet responsible enough to keep ourselves safe. Of course you wouldn't want to expose yourself to someone you feel abused by, but at the same time it's important to find a way to communicate that's honest and authentic, for the health of your own being.

Just as we need to learn to sit in the discomfort of our angry feelings, we also need to do so with our sadness and other feelings. A mindfulness practice will help you do this.

- LOW-THRESHOLD SADNESS — *empty, ignored, left out, miserable, vulnerable, confused, under the weather, emotional, misunderstood*
- HIGH-THRESHOLD SADNESS — *full-blown grief such as profound loss, despair, melancholy, defeated, crushed*

3. Hurt

Hurt is one of the more confusing feelings. The reason for this is that hurt, again according to some theorists, is an emotion and not a feeling. We are not born with hurt. Hurt is a combination of two feelings, sadness and fear. Remember we are born with four feelings: Mad, Sad, Glad and Bad. We are intrinsically hard-wired with those feelings as part of our DNA — everything else is an emotion. I have included hurt as part of our feeling compass because almost no one with an anger control issue has any idea how to process their hurt. In other words, they don't know how to deal with the combination of sadness and fear that manifests as hurt. I was already in my 30s before I was able to distinguish between sadness and fear. I realized that a lot of my anger stemmed from feeling sad and scared, but I was never able to express either specifically. So for me it was liberating to give myself permission to feel my hurt, to befriend it, turn it into an ally, and when I felt hurt to say to others, 'I feel sad or scared.'

- LOW-THRESHOLD HURT — *confused, overwhelmed, troubled, discouraged, ignored, left out, rejected, condemned, cheated, divided, odd, pressured*
- HIGH-THRESHOLD HURT — *dominated, exasperated, frantic, imposed upon, troubled, weepy, bad, bullied*

4. SCARED

Scared is another word for fear and is one of the major triggers for anger. According to Susan Jeffers, author of *Feel the Fear and Do It Anyway*, whenever we experience fear we are feeding ourselves the negative message 'I can't handle it' — meaning that whatever life is throwing at us right now, we cannot manage or be with it. It terrifies us so much that we either run like crazy or we get defensive and slip into attack mode and start fighting our corner. It's a fight–flight response to get us out of the discomfort or distress we are feeling.

To manage our anger we need to befriend our fears, we need to emotionally acclimatize ourselves to fear. Fear can become the best ally we have, because when faced with it we are reminded of our humanity and it asks us to push past the thresholds that limit us. Fear keeps us stuck and limited in our capacity to be fully human and embrace our lives in creative and strategic ways. By embracing our fear — 'feeling the fear and doing it anyway' – we build emotional resilience and this leads to being courageous. This eventually translates into healthy self-esteem, with which we build confidence in ourselves and others.

'It's not money that makes the world go round, it's fear.' The media constantly sells the need to insure ourselves against catastrophe, which is reinforced by negative news. It keeps us scared and in a continuous state of high alert, ever ready to defend or tackle the next misfortune. If we have a healthy dialogue with our internal driving fears we can control most of our 'shooting from the hip' reactions. The greatest antidote to fear is trust – both trusting ourselves and trusting others (see page 70).

- LOW-THRESHOLD FEAR – *ambivalent, anxious, bored, confused, dubious, distracted, jealous, feeling low, nervous, uneasy, unsettled, tentative, restless, strange*
- HIGH-THRESHOLD FEAR – *betrayed, distraught, horrible, intimidated, hysterical, overwhelmed, panicked, persecuted, petrified, shocked, threatened, trapped*

5. Peaceful

Feeling peaceful is not dissimilar to being tranquil. The more you pay attention to yourself and your surroundings, the more peace and tranquillity you will generate. People from all walks of life and cultures attend our courses and in order to honour the men and women from the Far East whose ancestors have been meditating and living mindfully for over 5,000 years, I included 'peaceful' in our feeling compass, as it is a term very familiar to them. One man from India expressed feeling 'tranquil' at different times during the course. In all the years I have been running groups I have never heard a Westerner refer to themselves as feeling tranquil.

As course participants explore the full range of the feeling compass, they begin to understand and make sense of their inner landscape. Developing their ability to articulate a broader range of feelings, they naturally begin to feel more relaxed, peaceful and tranquil. It's as if they've discovered huge chunks of information about themselves that they've never been privy to before. It's only through being still, paying attention to themselves and listening to others that a calm mind can be brought to a situation.

At the end of a programme, many participants have stated that they've not felt calm and peaceful in years, yet even after two days they are sleeping better. The more at peace you feel, the deeper you will sleep. Being at peace with oneself is like coming home. The more you know yourself and accept your humanity and limitations, the less you have to push for, fight or defend. There is a natural surrendering to what is. Accepting what is does not mean you are dis-empowered.

* EMOTIONAL WORDS THAT DESCRIBE PEACEFUL – *blissful, calm, contented, relaxed, settled, feeling at one with the universe, connected, free, liberated*

6. Powerful

Feeling powerful or empowered is often expressed at the end of a weekend or ten-week programme. Knowledge is power and being attentive, present, mindful, aware, open and receptive to new ideas often leaves people feeling more empowered to manage their lives. Impulsive and compulsive anger saps your vitality and leaves you feeling powerless – I often say that every time you express your anger inappropriately, you give your power away. Every time you manage to express your anger cleanly by remaining contained yet assertive, you empower yourself. People frequently leave our programmes staggered that they feel empowered enough to control their anger and, by so doing, become more powerful in their lives. Like the word 'peaceful', I included the word 'powerful' because it represents the multicultural aspect of this work. It honours the men and women from the plains of South America and Africa. These people often come from an agricultural background where they are familiar with their bodies being strong, formidable and powerful.

Feeling powerful is more like a body sensation. It's that feeling you get after a strong workout from exercise – you feel powerful and capable in your body. Translated into the field of feelings, it would be the opposite to feeling emotionally crushed or bankrupt. Discovering new insights, language and skills about themselves, people often leave our programmes feeling powerful, happy and peaceful.

- EMOTIONAL WORDS THAT DESCRIBE POWERFUL — *strong, resilient, positive, healthy, alert, bold, brave, capable, inspired, hopeful, pleased, proud, rewarded, satisfied, valued, vital, wonderful*

7. HAPPY

Being happy or joyful is often found in people who have the ability not to sweat the small stuff. People who are attentive and mindful and live in the present know what it means to be happy. The more relaxed you are, the easier and more natural it is for you to feel happy — remember that holiday feeling! Contrary to popular desire, happiness is not something that just befalls us — it has to be worked on. As we have seen, if you want to experience more happiness in your life you have to let go of your attachments and expectations. If you can do this, you will be less invested in the end result and therefore create less suffering.

This opens you up to experience more joy in your life, as each opportunity is a moment of creative spontaneity as opposed to trying to control an outcome to go your way. It takes time, understanding, reflection and patience to cultivate, but if you really think about it we have all the time in the world to grow beyond our self-limiting beliefs. As long as we commit to being mindful of our intentions and aware of our potential, and work with our limitations, we can also allow ourselves to experience joy. Sometimes, the reminder is just about absorbing all the moments of joy that cross our paths.

I remember a girlfriend of mine saying to me once, 'Michael, you wouldn't know happiness even if it was sitting on top of your head.' I have never forgotten that comment, because at the time it was true. I was so unhappy it was impossible for me to even think about what it meant to be happy. I was just surviving from one day to the next, desperately trying to avoid any feelings. It was a dark period of my life, and looking back, I realize how far I have come and what I have learnt and it makes me happy to be able to say it's possible!

* EMOTIONAL WORDS THAT DESCRIBE HAPPY — *pleasant, brilliant, excellent, fantastic, joyful, thrilled, excited, chirpy*

8. SHAME OR EMBARRASSED

A sense of shame or embarrassment is one of the major triggers for anger. So many people who suffer from anger also suffer from shame and I refer to it as self-defence anger. It is such a silent driving force and so often unrecognized that I can be bold enough to say that 95 per cent of people who attend our programmes suffer from it.

Guilt is 'I have made a mistake and I feel embarrassed about it and will make sure that I do some kind of make-up or just apologise for the mistake.'

Shame is 'I am a mistake. I am the rotten apple in the basket and, if you really knew what I was like, you would not like me, in fact you would not even be in my life because I am such a bad person.' That is called toxic shame.

The Feeling Compass Process

To develop self-awareness regarding your feelings, especially if you are concerned about the more uncomfortable ones you might be feeling right now, ask yourself the following:

1. *What am I feeling in the here and now?*

Sad, angry, hurt, scared, peaceful, powerful, happy, shame or a combination of feelings?

NOTE WHICH FEELINGS YOU ARE FEELING IN YOUR JOURNAL.

2. *What is triggering the feeling(s) right now?*

a. Memories of past events?
b. Concerns about the future?
c. Anything else?

3. *What demands (if any) am I placing on myself right now, or are being placed on me, that are triggering these feelings?*

a. Is there anything I need to attend to urgently this minute?
b. Is there anything I can really do at all?
c. Can I allow myself to feel these feelings without trying to change them?

4. *If there are no demands, what can I focus my attention on right now?*

I can focus my attention on what is positive in my life right now.

SUMMARIZE YOUR RESPONSE INTO A SHORT PARAGRAPH AND NOTE IT IN YOUR JOURNAL.

LOVING KINDNESS MEDITATION

1. Find a quiet place where you can sit comfortably. Keep your back and head up straight, feet firmly planted on the floor, and hands resting gently in your lap.

2. Once you are comfortable, take your attention to your breath. Take a couple of deep breaths into your abdomen and stay focused on your breathing for two minutes.

3. Now take your attention to your heart.

4. Place your hand on your heart and say, 'Love…love…love…, may my heart be filled with love.' Repeat this gently and softly to yourself. Connect to the words and what they mean to you. As you repeat them, imagine who you might say this to. Let an image of that person emerge.

5. Allow yourself to feel the warmth and love, and notice where you connect to it in your body. Experience yourself being caring, loving and tender. Allow yourself to feel the healing and soothing qualities of your feelings. Let it wash over you and gently repeat to yourself with clear intent: • *May I be well, healthy and strong* • *May I be happy* • *May I feel safe and secure* • *May I abide in peace* • *May I feel loved and cared for.*

6. Now slowly and gently bring to mind someone who is significant in your life, someone very important to you, someone you care for. Embrace them with your love and kindness, see them taking in your warmth. Visualize them smiling and happy. Now repeat the same lines you told yourself: • *May you be well, healthy and strong* • *May you be happy* • *May you feel safe and secure* • *May you abide in peace* • *May you feel loved and cared for.*

Take a deep breath, let these feelings wash over you and become aware of what you are experiencing.

7. Now bring another person who is equally significant into your awareness and repeat the same lines.

8. Now do this process with an acquaintance – preferably someone you barely know.

9. Move on to someone who triggered your anger either today or in the recent past.

10. Now do this with a person by whom you have felt hurt, or someone you are anxious about meeting in the near future.

11. Take another deep breath, do this a few times and then begin to radiate your love, tenderness and warmth to the people in your life. Take your attention to people in your neighbourhood and then in your town/city, to everyone in your area, and country, to everyone in the whole wide world. At this point, you can expand your attention as far as you desire, to include the living world and the wonderful universe we live in.

12. Finally, take a deep breath in and out slowly while bringing your attention back to yourself. Allow whatever you are feeling to fill your whole being, notice how peaceful and relaxed you are feeling. Breathing in peacefully, breathing out peacefully, be at peace with yourself and with the world.

In your own time, and when you are ready, open your eyes and make a few notes in your journal. I would suggest you do this meditation at least every other day for a few weeks. If you are feeling angry with someone and are not able to shift your anger towards them, this meditation can often do the job.

ANGER MEDITATION

This meditation has been compared with the experience of hitting a patch of ice while driving your car. As your car starts to skid out of control, your natural instinct is to try to manoeuvre out of the skid, but this will make the situation worse. The best way of dealing with it is not to turn away, but to turn into the skid and allow the car to come to a natural stop. To put it slightly differently, trying to move away can put you in more danger, but allowing yourself just to go with the flow can help you regain control and reach a safer conclusion.

With this Anger Meditation, instead of trying to control the situation or repress your angry feelings, you will be facing them head-on. You will just go with the intensity of the feelings, respectfully, rather than resisting them and pushing them away.

If you want this process to work for you, you will need firstly to agree with yourself not to vent or act out your anger while doing this exercise, and for a short while afterwards.

It's possible you might even feel more angry than usual at first, as you become more connected to your anger. This is often an indication that it is emerging and coming closer to the surface.

By combining three aspects of yourself – your awareness, your breath and your anger – you bring each of these vital components into a respectful harmony with each other.

1. Anger often has a physical dimension to it. See if you can notice where you might be feeling the anger in your body.

2. Don't think about the cause of it or what has triggered it. Just notice where it's located in your body and if it has some sort of texture or colour to it. It might even have a particular sound or a smell. Does it feel hot or cold?

3. Don't think about the source of the anger or what has triggered it. Stay focused on its underlying aspects.

4. Begin to breathe slowly and deeply and, as you inhale, allow your breath to connect to the anger you are experiencing inside your body.

5. Allow the contact to be tentative at first.

6. Keep breathing and, as you do so, gradually allow there to be less distance between your anger and your breath.

7. Let your awareness embrace the anger in your body and your breath — remain centred in yourself.

8. Stay focused and it's possible you will notice your anger become more tolerable and stable.

9. Notice that you are managing to handle the intensity of whatever it is you are feeling.

10. As you do this, actually welcome your anger as part of you — which it is. As you befriend your anger, it becomes your teacher, not your enemy, not something to get rid of.

This exercise may give you an insight into your 'anger triggers' and allow you to see your part in an angry incident. The hope for the future is that you will use this insight and express your feelings in more considered and respectful ways.

I keep reminding members of my groups that the idea is not to become a saint or an idealized image of a 'peaceful person' — it is to make friends with whatever you are feeling and be at peace with it.

CHAPTER FOUR

EMBRACING THE POLARITIES IN LIFE

In the context of our lives, polarity is the relationship between opposed entities, such as good and evil. The most effective way of embracing polarities in your life is to keep your heart open, no matter what. The impulsive mind might think it's impossible to keep your heart open in a fit of anger, but eventually, and with practice, you will find that it is indeed possible to be enraged and empathetic towards the other person at the same time — even though the intensity of your feelings might get the better of you in the beginning.

A Fixed Viewpoint

Reaching a point where we can agree to disagree and allow another person to have their experience is to begin to embrace duality. There will always be another way, different from our way. It doesn't make us right or wrong. It's just a different perspective, a different position.

MANY OF OUR COURSE ATTENDEES are individuals who see the world from a fixed viewpoint – no wonder they're angry, when the world around them gets it so wrong so often! Sometimes it's not even about being right, but simply a compulsive need to take up an oppositional and defiant position. They enjoy the drama and intensity of the adrenalized moment of friction. To continually force other people to conform to their rules, to condemn them when they don't, to criticize them for seeing the world differently is to create an endless stream of conflict. This communication style winds people up, eventually triggering their anger.

Expanding Our View

Often our way of perceiving the world is incredibly limited. We are taught to think in terms of right or wrong, good or bad, positive or negative, should and shouldn't, 'us and them', and all this creates a lot of suffering for humanity. We could go as far as saying that we think 'in opposition'. No wonder there is so much conflict in the world today!

The mind experiences the world in a linear way. It's impossible for the ego to transcend duality because the ego sees the world through the lens of 'us and them'. Its sole purpose is to protect and it does this by categorizing.

The heart, on the other hand, does not experience the world in duality – the heart sees the world as 'one' and naturally embraces diversity. It does not see or relate to the world as 'us and them', it just expands and accepts what is. I believe that is why Buddhism has never faded into historical obscurity and has become increasingly popular in the West. It moves away from the either/or paradigm and embraces the both/and paradigm. Shifting into a position of acceptance with ourselves and others frees us from the ongoing ego battles that many of us endure on a daily basis. The emphasis is to live in a realm of harmony rather than one of constant friction. Being in harmony with ourselves, people and the world is profoundly healing and brings a feeling of being connected and at one.

Accepting What 'Is'

The capacity to accept what 'is' without trying to change it is a highly effective strategy in controlling anger. I have been introducing this idea of embracing polarities to course participants for many years now, encouraging them not to get caught up in having to take up a position of – usually – moral superiority. It's fascinating to watch how they either accept it or have tremendous resistance to it.

One of the rules I use in my anger management courses is: 'It's okay to have a different opinion.' Opinions are not facts – everyone's reality is different and everyone's reality is subjective. You might need to remind yourself of this when you're next in a compromising position. Accepting what 'is' in our culture is virtually impossible because we have been educated to be competitive from a very early age; by our very nature we strive to get ahead and are sensitized to being right or wrong, winning or losing. It is so hard to accept what 'is' when our nature is to take the moral high ground, to be right no matter what, to win and take no prisoners, to be ahead of the game. This is amplified and exaggerated in hotheads.

Is It Really Worth It?

Think about how many arguments you get yourself into because you are hell-bent on being right. When someone accuses you of being wrong, have you noticed how it gets your back up and how you take it personally? How many ego battles have you endured because you're determined to be seen as being right, even when you know you're actually wrong – but you continue to fight the battle for the pure sadistic joy of making your opponent suffer even more? Admit it, there are some of you who simply love crossing swords, the taste of blood and the smell of burnt flesh around you. There's an attractive sense of power in it. In that moment, you feel invincible and omnipotent.

The question you could ask yourself is: has it ever been really worth it? Every argument we encounter can reduce our life force by a few hours, days or even weeks, depending on the intensity. We forget that being right is subjective – somewhere else on the planet it could be interpreted as wrong.

If you didn't live in the confines of being right or wrong, how different would your life be? In the research I've done over five years, I found that 60 per cent of people thought that if duality did not exist there would be pure chaos, and 40 per cent considered it would lead to liberation. What do you think? If we had to remove duality from our lives, do you imagine your life would get better or worse?

Allowing Without Judgement

When a person asks me a question such as 'Do you think it's right or wrong to tell my wife to stop crying when I think she's trying to manipulate me?', I often reply, 'Perhaps this is not about right or wrong but about your own discomfort in seeing your wife expressing her sadness or anger because you are not taking her needs seriously. Instead of wondering whether it's right or wrong, you could maybe think about what is getting in the way of you being compassionate and empathetic.' The danger occurs when we attach judgements, values, morals and beliefs to our thoughts.

The Bigger Picture

For many people with anger issues, it's inconceivable to consider living without rigid ego boundaries reinforcing duality and justifying these 'self-destructive structures' because it serves as a moral compass. Another golden rule of anger management is: 'Stop, think and take a look at the bigger picture.'

This means looking at situations from a wide variety of different perspectives:

- *Considering the other person's valid reality*
- *Being compassionate and empathetic*
- *Widening your viewpoint and learning to accept each other's limitations*
- *Thinking about every eventuality and being mindful of your impact*
- *Recognizing that the other person might be reflecting parts of you that you hide, deny or repress.*

It's so hard to be bigger than the situation when we feel we're not being treated fairly or are accused of something we didn't do or say – but herein lies the point. To remain focused on the bigger picture, you have to value the health of yourself and your family or community more than your desire to be seen as right. If we can shift our attention from satisfying our need to win, to hold on to our position or to seek approval, we allow something else to define the health and wealth of our relationships. I call it humility, and from this place our humanity emerges. We recognize that we are not that different from each other, that our fundamental needs are the same and that we're in this boat together.

Every time we are responsible for hurting another, we hurt ourselves. True power comes from empowering people, not disempowering them.

The Path to Integrity

In the Buddha's Noble Eightfold Path (see page 128), he talks about right view, right intention, right speech, right action, right livelihood, right effort, right mindfulness and right connection. In this context, 'right' means demonstrating integrity in everything we say, do, think and feel. When we live with integrity, our actions, behaviours, thoughts and feelings are aligned to the greater good of mankind. There is peace to be found in following the Noble Eightfold Path.

Finding the middle path in all our actions, remaining constant and living our lives with integrity is a way to experience peace and tranquillity.

Don't Take This Personally…

Another way we can remain objective and open to the bigger picture is to stop taking things personally and allow others their point of view. Every time you take personally what someone else says to you, you create personal suffering.

> ### The Buddha's Noble Eightfold Path
>
> **RIGHT VIEW** – Seeing situations from a broader perspective.
>
> **RIGHT INTENTION** – Living with integrity and having a healthy moral compass.
>
> **RIGHT SPEECH** – Having a clear understanding of the power of words, how they can hurt and how they can heal.
>
> **RIGHT ACTION** – Being clear about how our actions can affect others in healthy or unhealthy ways.
>
> **RIGHT LIVELIHOOD** – Making sure our career choices and occupation do not harm others in any way.
>
> **RIGHT EFFORT** – Our ability to recognize that everything takes effort in order to succeed, but too much effort can harm us and too little effort will not get the task done.
>
> **RIGHT MINDFULNESS** – Paying attention to everything we say, do, think and feel.
>
> **RIGHT CONNECTION** – Allowing ourselves to connect in ways that harm neither ourselves nor others.

I was one of those people who took everything that anyone said to me personally. I would use any criticism to beat myself up and reinforce what a bad person I was. I heard their feedback as 'You have a flawed character' – and of course my only way of dealing with that was to respond by feeling ashamed or defending myself in anger. The way I trained myself to stop taking things personally was to ask my staff, family and friends, when they observed me reacting to situations whether on the phone or in the company of others, to simply remind me with one question: 'Michael, are you taking what the other person is saying to you personally?' This enabled me to become more attentive and mindful of the moment and situation and served as a reminder that taking what others said personally was an effective way of keeping my suffering alive. It was like adding fuel to an inner fire that burnt me way beyond the intention of any comment I received.

A Question of Interpretation
I had to remind myself continually that I needed to hear the comment, the feedback or the criticism and ask myself what I made that mean to me. I needed to step back and reflect on why someone would say that to me. I had to question whether they were projecting their own insecurities on to me or were providing an opportunity for me to look deeper within myself and reflect on their meaning.

Giving yourself time to step back and look at the bigger picture, becoming mindful of how you may be interpreting someone's actions, means you can become clearer about the suffering you may be inflicting upon yourself – and therefore choose to stop it. Instead of mindless self-sabotage, you can choose mindful and responsible action or non-action.

Negative Core Beliefs

If influential people in our lives say negative things to us when we are very young, at some point in our development we introject those comments (swallow them whole) and they become our core beliefs about ourselves, the internal voices in our head, our inner judge, policeman, critic – our demons.

OUR INNER CRITIC SERVES as a reminder that to remain safe and out of harm's way we need to behave and act in a certain manner in order to be loved and accepted by others. But at some point you must ask if that is really true of you today or if your internal voices now serve only to beat you up, imprison and suffocate you.

Practising mindfulness teaches you to become increasingly aware of your inner state of being and thoughts. Think about how many negative thoughts you have about yourself on a daily basis – for example, thoughts like 'Pull yourself together, don't be so stupid, grow up, stop being a loser, you are seriously thick, etc...' But once you get the hang of the different mindfulness meditations, you can slowly and with discipline begin to eliminate the toxic noise of your inner critic. Generally these voices remind us constantly that we're useless or bad, a waste of time or space, or that we were born a failure or should not have been born at all. They drown out any positive, supporting, kind or encouraging voice. Negative voices are like phantoms in the night, they come and go at random, and usually only become active when we're feeling stressed, insecure, overwhelmed, confused or uncomfortable. They never seem to be around when we're feeling peaceful, happy, contented and relaxed. Becoming mindful of these negative voices and challenging them, instead of allowing them to run riot in your head, will eventually take the charge out of them.

Basically, once you recognize that your negative internal thoughts have a lot more to say to you than anybody else, you'll find that the world really isn't out to get you and you won't feel the need to keep hiding or defending yourself. Taking things personally is something angry people do – it's second nature to them – but if you stop taking things personally you can reduce your anger by at least 60 per cent.

This is not to say you'll never get angry, but you'll be a lot less trigger-happy. Instead of jumping to conclusions about what you think people are saying about you, you can delay your reaction and question what exactly they mean. Are they really trying to undermine you or are they trying to make a point that will in fact allow you to evolve into the person you actually are?

Taking things personally is something angry people do – it's second nature to them...

JOURNAL TASK

Let's see if we can pull out some negative core beliefs you may have rambling around in your head. Write a list in your journal of the things you take personally – for example, when you feel that someone is criticizing you or challenging you for not taking responsibility for something that had to be done.

Now work out what *you make these things mean to you*. Next, write down the negative core belief that stands out the most. My example is, 'However hard I try, I can never get anything right and that usually makes me believe I'm a failure.'

Close your eyes and give yourself permission to get present. Take the time you need. Now ask yourself a question based on the negative core belief. For instance, in my case I ask myself, 'Am I a failure?' Then notice if any other negative voices become active in your head. If they do, notice what they do next and allow them just to be there. Gently ask those voices to be still for a moment and remind them that you're doing the best you can right now and that there is no longer a place for them in your life. Once upon a time they served you well and may even have protected you, but today they stifle and block your creativity. Kindly ask them to leave.

You can see a detailed demonstration of this process on *www.angermindfulness.co.uk*.

The Art of Communication

People are not always expert communicators and can be clumsy in their choice of words. The best way to avoid the consequences of jumping to the wrong conclusion is to check out what people really mean — we so often assume things that are way off the reality mark.

This is where sitting in the discomfort of our feelings and delaying gratification really pays off. Instead of jumping down someone's throat with a tomahawk in hand, make sure you understand what the other person is actually trying to say. This way you spare everyone unnecessary conflict and you prevent your inner demons contaminating your own and another's reality. Sitting with your own inner process at the same time as remaining open and objective towards someone else's perspective — embracing the polarities — is a life skill worth cultivating and offers tremendous value.

We always have to bear in mind, of course, that the other person/s might also be emotionally challenged in that moment. It's useful to approach a difficult situation by considering possible solutions.

Consider the following:
- What might be going on for the other person right now?
- How are they feeling in this moment?
- What do they need from me now?
- How can I be of service to them in this situation?

It takes courage to sit in our discomfort, but by creating space for ourselves and remaining objective it becomes easier to relate to the other person as a human (who is also finding it difficult) rather than demonizing them and turning them into the enemy. Try stepping into their shoes and feeling what *they're* feeling. If things start hotting up, you can immediately choose to cool them down. By training yourself to tune in to your feelings regularly, you can begin to apply mindfulness to these stressful situations, so that you can slow down, take stock, and react in a more creative way when confronted with a tense situation. The more you are able to do this, the more empowered you will be to control your anger. When you become mindful, everyone around you will benefit.

Listening Skills

When you're angry, listening skills go out the window because it becomes more important to be the first one to get your point across. When we are mindful, we are more open to another's subjective experience and perspective and our ability to really listen and not interrupt increases.

For me, listening is everything when it comes to clear communication and developing healthy relationships with oneself and others. And if you allow yourself to listen, you might surprise yourself and hear something you've never heard before! I find some of the poorest listeners I have ever met are the angry heads. I often have to remind participants in my groups and one-to-one work to just listen without interrupting. For many it's the hardest task to commit to, but by doing so they discover new things about themselves every day.

Also, it's easier to listen and be heard if you're not speaking too fast. When people speak too fast they land up talking over their feelings. Talking too fast or interrupting all the time does not allow you to sink into your feelings and feel what you are either hearing or thinking.

Manage Your Expectations

Managing your expectations is the final ingredient in becoming adept at holding the tension in any situation. Once you become mindful of how attached you are to a particular outcome or to winning and can learn to let this go, managing your expectations follows naturally. According to John Lee, author of *Facing the Fire*, expectations are unrealized resentments just waiting to happen. Having high expectations of yourself and others can lead to a lot of heartache, and lowering your expectations allows you to be able to work towards achieving the goal. It's okay to hold a high expectation, but it's not okay to criticize, shame, blame or demonize either yourself or another when the goal is not met. Lowering the bar allows for mistakes, and mistakes remind us of what it means to be human.

Becoming Your Own Teacher

Every time a person triggers your anger, in that very moment they potentially become your guru or teacher. They are offering you the opportunity to embrace the polarities in yourself and to view the world from an entirely different perspective.

MINDFULNESS TEACHES us to hold all possibilities and to be open to those we haven't even considered. Instead of demonizing other people whenever you feel threatened, remember that they're giving you an opportunity to embody mindfulness practice, expand your awareness and become present to the moment. They offer you great insight into your own limitations. At the end of the day, our own egos are our biggest enemy and threat to ourselves and to the world.

One Last Lesson

In his book *Vinegar into Honey*, Ron Leifer makes some excellent points about why we get so angry. A very important point is that anger is fuelled by our desires and also at times by our

---

'No one saves us but ourselves. No one can and no one may. We ourselves must walk the path.'

BUDDHA

---

aversions and our self-interests. There are three simple questions we need to ask ourselves when our anger is triggered.

QUESTION ONE
'What did I want that I did not get?'
This question is based on being fuelled by our desires.

QUESTION TWO
'What was I getting that I did not want?'
This question is based on what we have an aversion to.

QUESTION THREE
'How did I feel about myself?'
This question is based on self-interest.

Each of these questions allows us insight into our mischief, into how we find ourselves reacting to any form of discomfort, be it physical, emotional, psychological or spiritual. When you learn to become attentive not just to your needs, but to the needs of others as well, your ability to accommodate others becomes possible. As you become more present and emotionally available in your life, the need to catastrophize becomes less of an issue. Instead of overreacting, sweating the small stuff or turning everything into a drama, you allow yourself the internal space and time to deal with things in an emotionally mature and contained way. This nurtures your self-esteem and your overall sense of contentment. When you can eventually do that, you will be so much happier.

Continuing the Journey: Writing this book on anger and mindfulness has allowed me to relive a journey I started as a young person. From living in a state of depression and constant emotional suffering in my teenage and young adult years, I have grown to acknowledge and accept that life's continuous daily challenges have something to teach me about myself. Through learning to be mindful I have developed my capacity and deepened my understanding of what it means to sit in my own discomfort. This, together with the help of a solid theoretical model that has given me a concise communication skill with which to express my anger, has worked wonders for me. Of course, it has been a long and arduous journey that has involved many falling-outs and difficult lessons, but I have taken each learning and applied it and used it with heart to support other people along their path.

I expect your journey to be similar to my own, except that I have the added advantage of learning from the many people who come to my anger management classes. I hope that some of the insights and key learnings from doing this work for 20 years help you to identify with the material. Don't expect to arrive at your destination quickly – it will take time, practice and dedication to get there.

There is no doubt that a meditational practice enabled me to bring so much more awareness into my life. The beneficial impact of 15–45 minutes of meditation a day to effect change is profound. It has become the ground on which I base my days. Without this I believe the red mist that used to cloud my life would still have control. To say that my anger led me to stillness seems an outrageous, if not illogical statement – but it is true. It has finally become my friend.

Acknowledgements

Editing a book written by a person who is dyslexic is not an easy task. You have to know the person deeply to understand the mysterious mechanisms of their dyslexic mind. Manuela Viana has understood my ramblings and turned them into clear, concise passages with a particular talent for making some difficult concepts easy to understand. When at times I had gone off at a tangent, her understanding of the material got this book to a place that was digestible and thought-provoking at the same time. I believe Manuela is naturally mindful. She breathes mindfulness into everything she does. Without her specifically, it would not have been possible to write this book.

If it were not for the commissioning editor, Monica Perdoni, I would not be writing this book either. Monica, I appreciate you giving me the opportunity to take my life's work to the next level. Thank you for all your support you gave me along the way and for your encouraging emails.

Every time I sent a new chapter to the chief editor, Jayne Ansell, I always looked forward to her comments and changes. Jayne, thank you for encouraging me in the ways that you did. I hope I have done you proud.

I believe a book does not become a book until the copy editor has got her hands on it. Jenni Davis has done a marvellous job making sure that everything flowed and read as clearly and succinctly as it does.

Marina Cano, thank you for your support and patience and for guiding me into your sacred world of wildlife photography.

Jeremy McMinn and Lynne Willcock, thank you for holding the fort while we build a new platform.

Finally, the little buddhas in my life, Sage and Feather, are the two cats who live with me. They breathe stillness into my busy life of schedules and deadlines, constantly reminding me to slow down, breathe, stretch, take in the day and bask in a strip of sunshine whenever possible.

To you all, I salute you because, without you by my side, this book would not have been possible.

BIBLIOGRAPHY

Beating Anger: The Eight-Point Plan for Coping with Rage by Mike Fisher (Rider, 2005)

Facing the Fire: Experiencing and Expressing Anger Appropriately by John Lee and Bill Scott (Bantam Doubleday Bell, 1997)

Full Catastrophe Living: How to Cope with Stress, Pain and Illness using Mindfulness Meditation by Jon Kabat-Zinn (Piatkus, 2001)

Get Some Headspace: 10 Minutes Can Make All the Difference by Andy Puddicombe (Hodder & Stoughton, 2011)

Home Coming: Reclaiming and Championing Your Inner Child by John Bradshaw (Piatkus Books, 1999)

Mindfulness for Dummies by Shamash Alidina (John Wiley & Sons, 2010)

Nonviolent Communication: A Language of Life by Marshall B. Rosenberg (Puddle Dancer Press, 2003)

One to One: Self-Understanding through Journal Writing by Christina Baldwin (M. Evans & Co. Inc., 1977, updated 1991)

The Dark Side of the Light Chasers by Debbie Ford (Mobius, 2001)

The Mindful Manifesto: How Doing Less and Noticing More Can Help Us Thrive in a Stressed-Out World by Dr Jonty Heaversedge and Ed Halliwell (Hay House UK, 2010)

The Path of Mindfulness Meditation: Finding Balance in the Midst of Chaos: The Application of Mindfulness and Vipassana Meditation for Personal Transformation by Peter Strong (Outskirts Press, 2010)

The Power of Now by Eckhart Tolle (Hodder, 2001)

Vinegar into Honey: Seven Steps to Understanding and Transforming Anger, Aggression and Violence by Ron Leifer (Snow Lion Publications, 2008)

Wherever You Go, There You Are: Mindfulness Meditation for Everyday Life by Jon Kabat-Zinn (Piatkus, 2004)

Why Mars and Venus Collide: Improve Your Relationships by Understanding How Men and Women Cope Differently with Stress by John Gray (Harper Element, 2008)

Resources

UK

Alcoholics Anonymous, 0845 769 7555, *www.alcoholics-anonymous.org.uk*

Beating Anger – Anger Management, 0345 1300 286, *www.beatinganger.com*

British Association of Anger Management, 0345 1300 286, *www.angermanage.co.uk*

Mike Fisher (anger management specialist and counsellor), 07931 569051, *www.angermanage.co.uk*

National Domestic Violence Helpline (co-run by Women's Aid and Refuge), 0808 2000 247, *www.womensaid.org.uk*

Respect (aiming to increase the safety of those experiencing domestic violence), 0207 549 0578, *www.respect.uk.net*

Traumatic Incident Reduction (trauma therapy, Henry Whitfield), 0800 849 6723 or 0207 183 2485, *www.tir.org.uk*

United Kingdom Council for Psychotherapy (UKCP), 0207 014 9955, *www.psychotherapy.org.uk*

Women Within (women's personal development organization), 01423 864261, *www.transitionseurope.com*

Australia

ABC1 Making Australia Happy, *www.abc.net.au/tv/programs/making-australia-happy/*

Australia MiCBT Institute, +61 3 6224 7707, *www.mindfulness.net.au*

Be Mindful, *www.bemindful.com.au*

Mandy Lamkin (facilitator and trainer), *www.mindfulness.com.au/MandyBiog.htm*

Mindfulness Centre, +61 8 8272 0046, *www.mindfulnesscentre.com*

Mindfulness.org.au (sourcing mindulness courses in Australia), *www.mindfulness.org.au*

INDEX

accepting what 'is' 123–4
aggressive anger 21–4, 42
Anger meditation 118–19
angry feelings 106–7
anxiety 51, 63, 64–5, 68, 75, 77, 100
approval, seeking 76–80, 82, 126
apps 56
attachments 17, 19, 26, 27, 28, 31, 36, 39, 61, 113

balance 8–11
Baldwin, Christina 13
being present 35
bigger picture, the 53, 61, 126–9
Body Scan meditation 74, 91–5, 102
brain 29–31, 32, 60
Brown, Ralph P. 16
Buddha 8, 12, 82, 85, 127–8, 136
Buddhism 40, 41, 123

clearing the red mist 98–9
communication 72, 106–7, 133–5, 138
compassionate detachment 16–17, 36, 41
confidence 75, 81, 110
control, relinquishing 68–70, 80
core beliefs, negative 130–2

de-stressing 57, 61–85
  exercise 82–5
depression 9–10, 21, 40, 71, 77, 103, 138

ego identity 26, 28, 60
embarrassment 114
emotional language 44

emotions 103–4, 108
empathy 16, 17, 61, 125, 126
expectations 17, 18, 80, 92, 113, 135
exploders 20, 21–4, 54–5, 59, 77, 79, 103

fear 19, 21, 26, 27, 28, 42, 45, 63, 70, 72, 75, 100, 108, 109–10
  see also scared
feeling compass 103–14
  process 115
feelings 43–4
  disassociation 34, 43, 103
  emotions and 103–4, 108
  suppression 21, 22, 27, 44–6, 103
fight-or-flight response 29–30
freedom 9, 36, 75, 76

guilt 24, 105, 114

happiness 42–3, 45, 113–14
high arousal indicators 74
hotheads 25–6, 124
hurt 21, 27, 42, 44, 45, 71, 102, 103, 107, 108–9, 117, 127

imploders 20, 21, 22–3, 24, 26, 59, 77, 79, 103

Jacobson, Edmund 95
Jeffers, Susan 109
journal writing 13, 23, 24, 33, 35, 47, 57, 62, 71, 72, 76, 77, 82, 85, 91, 95, 99, 101, 115, 117, 132

142

Kübler-Ross, Elisabeth 52

Lawrence, D.H. 34–5
Lee, John 135
Leifer, Ron 136–7
listening 25, 47, 53, 61, 106–7, 111, 134–5
Loving Kindness meditation 105, 116–18

marketing 27, 37–8
meaning 28, 39, 41
media 27, 37–8, 110
mindfulness 16–19, 24, 30–1, 75, 130
Mindfulness meditation 32–3, 74, 101, 105

opinions 124

passive-aggressive anger 10, 20–1, 42
peaceful 44, 57, 88, 103, 110–11, 112, 117, 119, 131
Perls, Fritz 9, 75
post-traumatic stress disorder 52–3
powerful 37, 44, 103, 112–13
pressure, putting yourself under 79–80, 82
prioritizing your own life 66–8, 80
progressive muscle relaxation technique 95–7
proving yourself 53, 76–80, 82

react/respond 59–61
relaxation 51, 54–9
risk-taking 72, 76

sad 21, 27, 42, 44, 45, 102, 103, 107–8, 109, 125
scared 44, 101, 102, 103, 108, 109–10
see also fear
self-esteem 38, 65, 66–7, 68, 72, 75, 76, 77, 79, 81, 84, 110, 137
Shaking the Apple Tree 63–4, 66, 78, 82
shame 21, 26, 27, 42, 44, 45, 103, 105, 106, 114, 128, 135
silence 51–2, 53, 56, 85
solitude 50, 53, 54, 58, 85
stillness 50–3, 54, 56, 57, 58, 73, 85, 138
stress 50–1, 63, 66, 69, 80
   common effects 62
   self-esteem and 81
suffering 42–7, 63, 64, 84, 122, 128, 129, 138
survivors 25

taking things personally 26, 124, 128–9, 131, 132
Tolle, Eckhart 35–6, 75
trust 47, 69–76, 110
tuning in to yourself 52, 92, 93, 100, 101, 102, 105, 134

unconscious drives 64–5

vigilance 11, 100
   hyper-vigilance 73
volume control exercise 89–91

143